I AM GRATEFUL TO GOD FOR EVERYTHING! AND I BELIEVE THAT THE MEANING OF LIFE IS TO MAKE SENSE OF OTHER LIVES. D.P., YOU ARE THE MEANING OF MY LIFE.
LOV U

ANDRÉ PALIN DE MORAES

2024

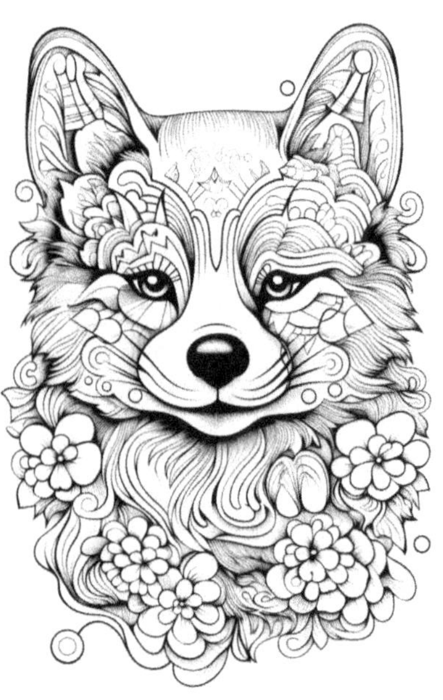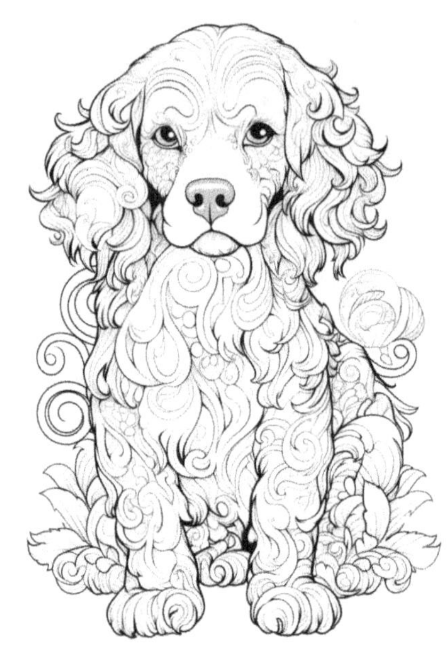

This Book Belongs to:

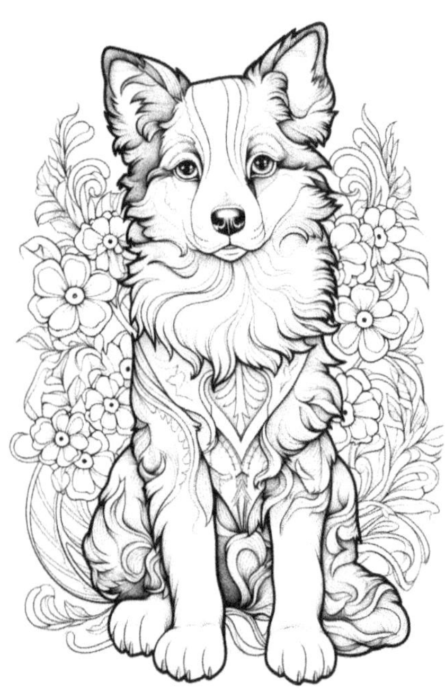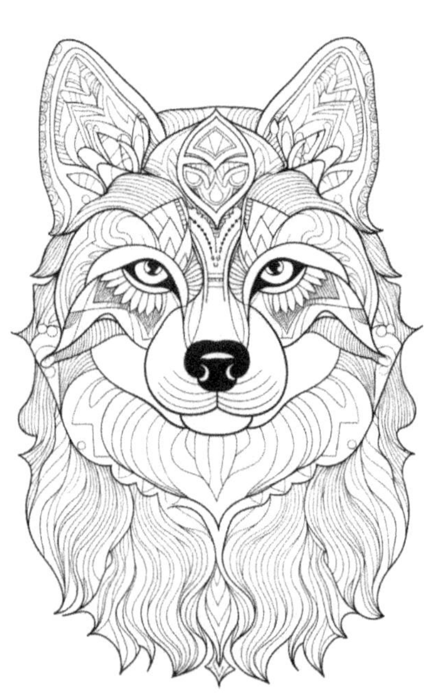

Test Color Page

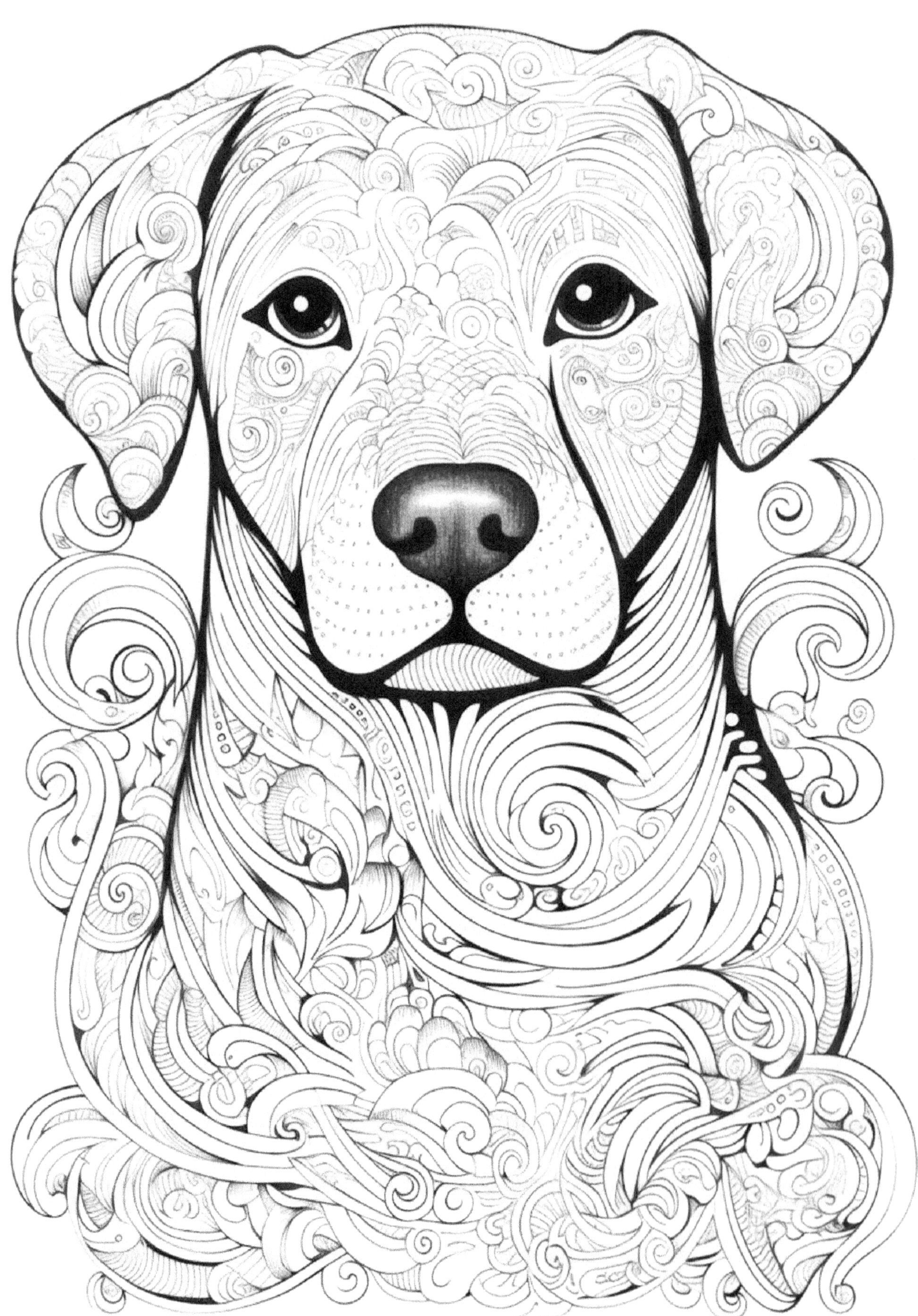

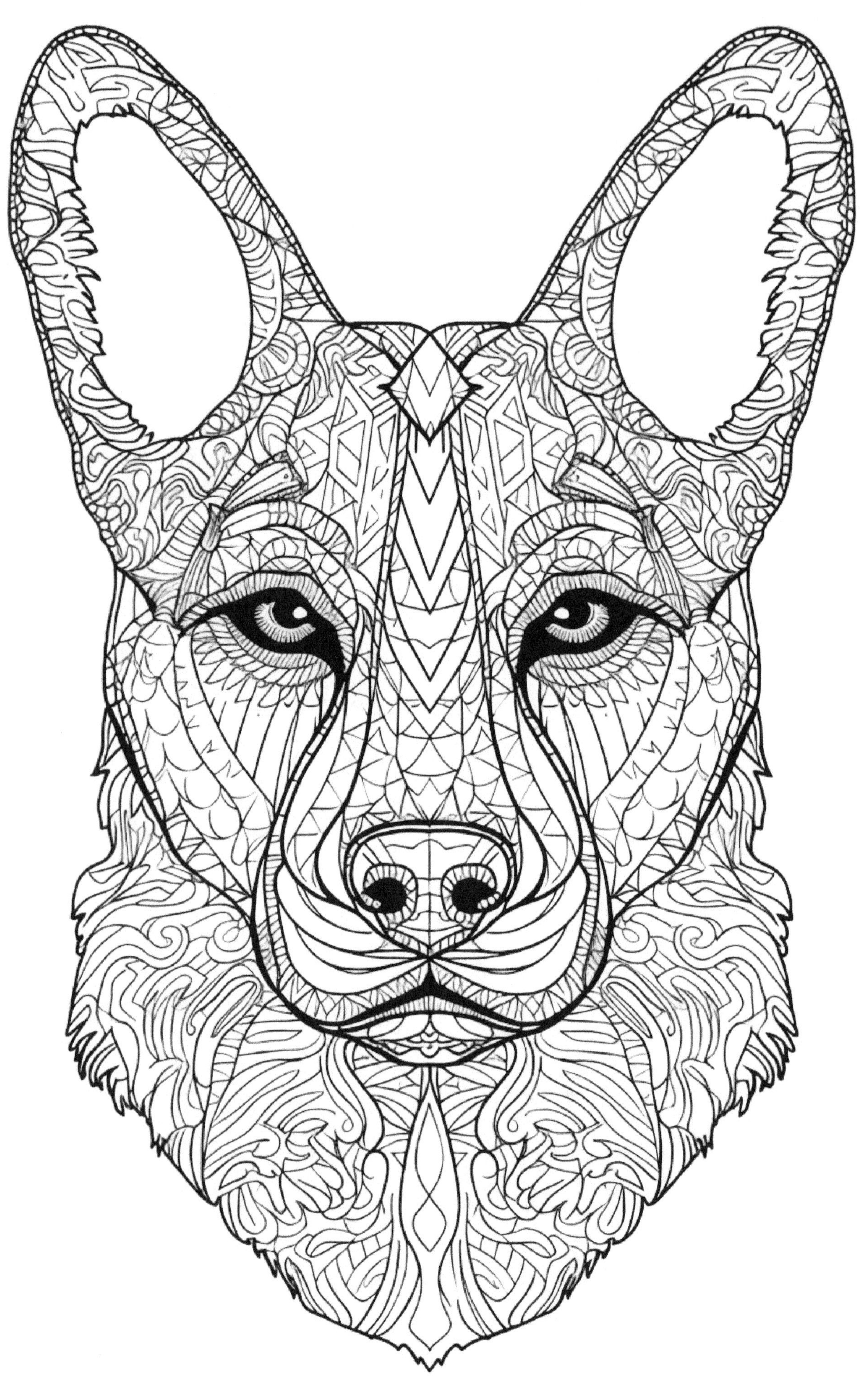

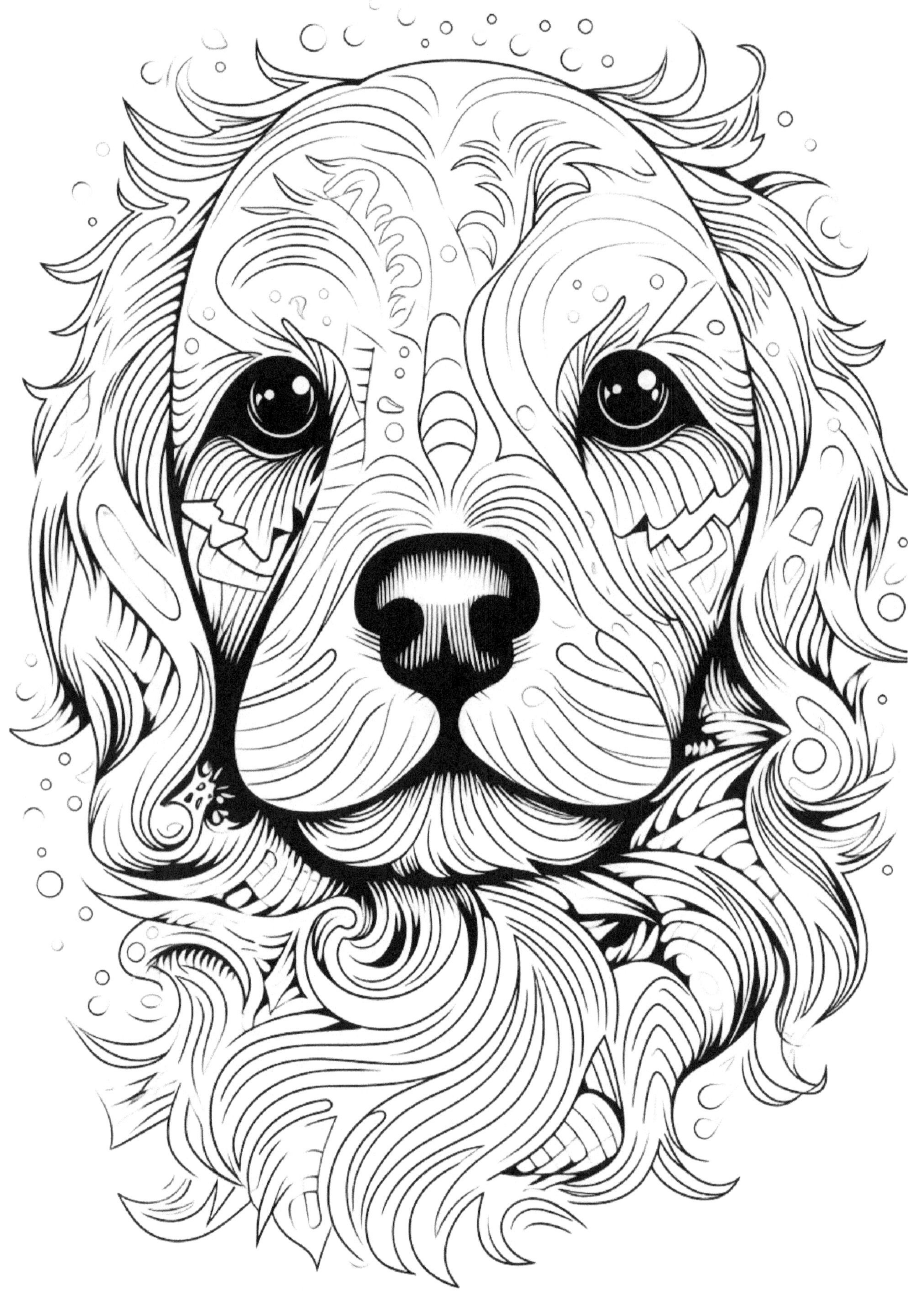

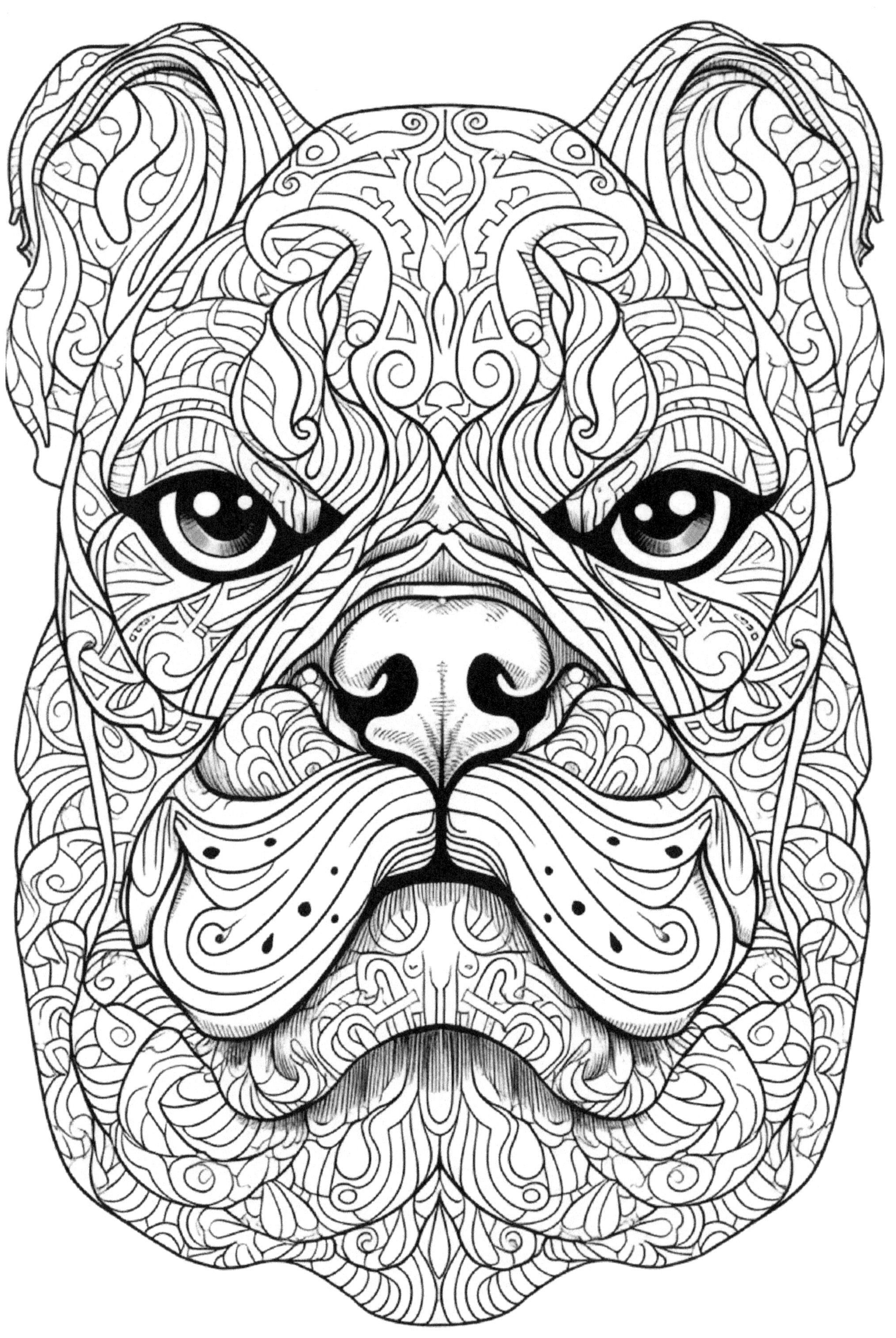

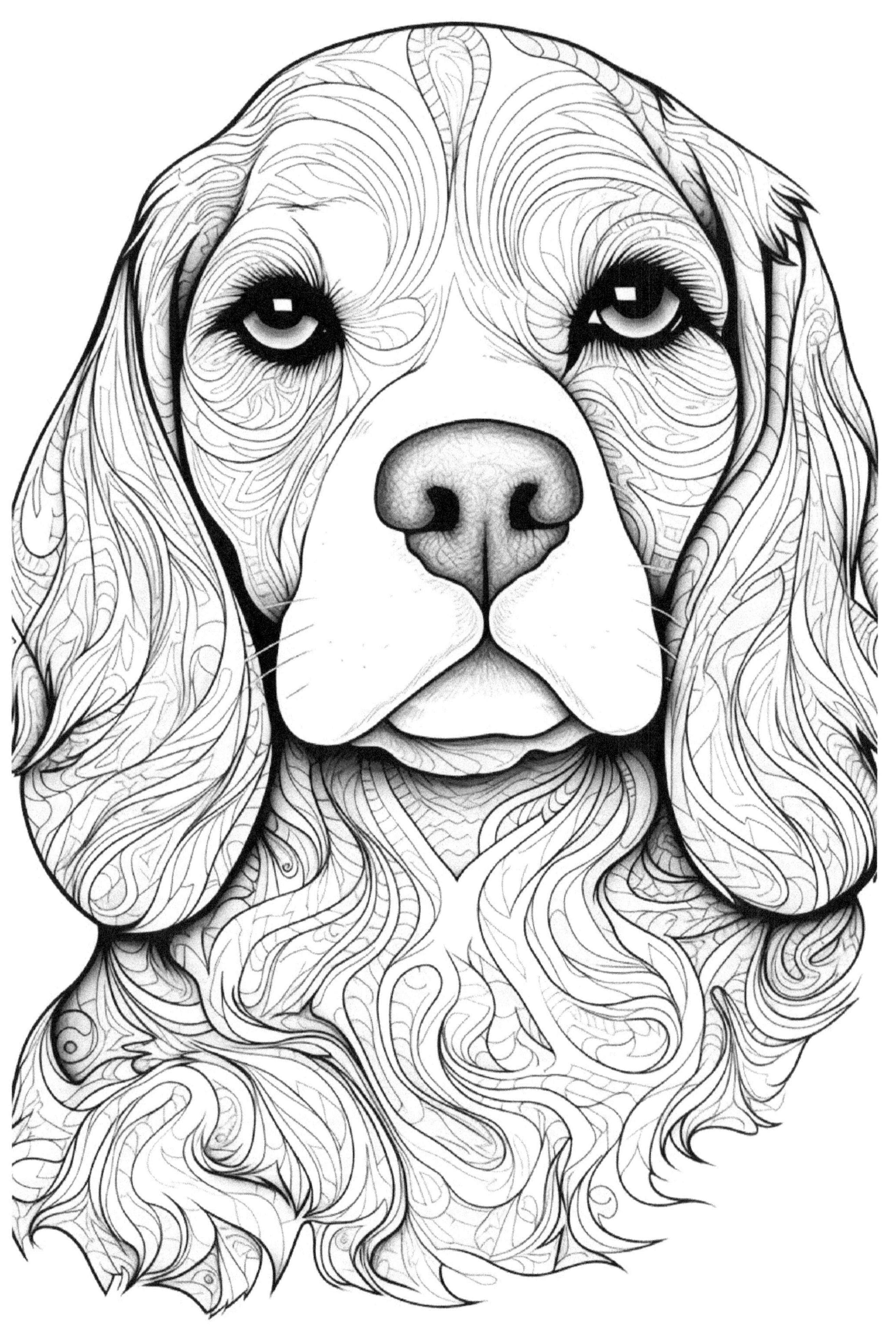

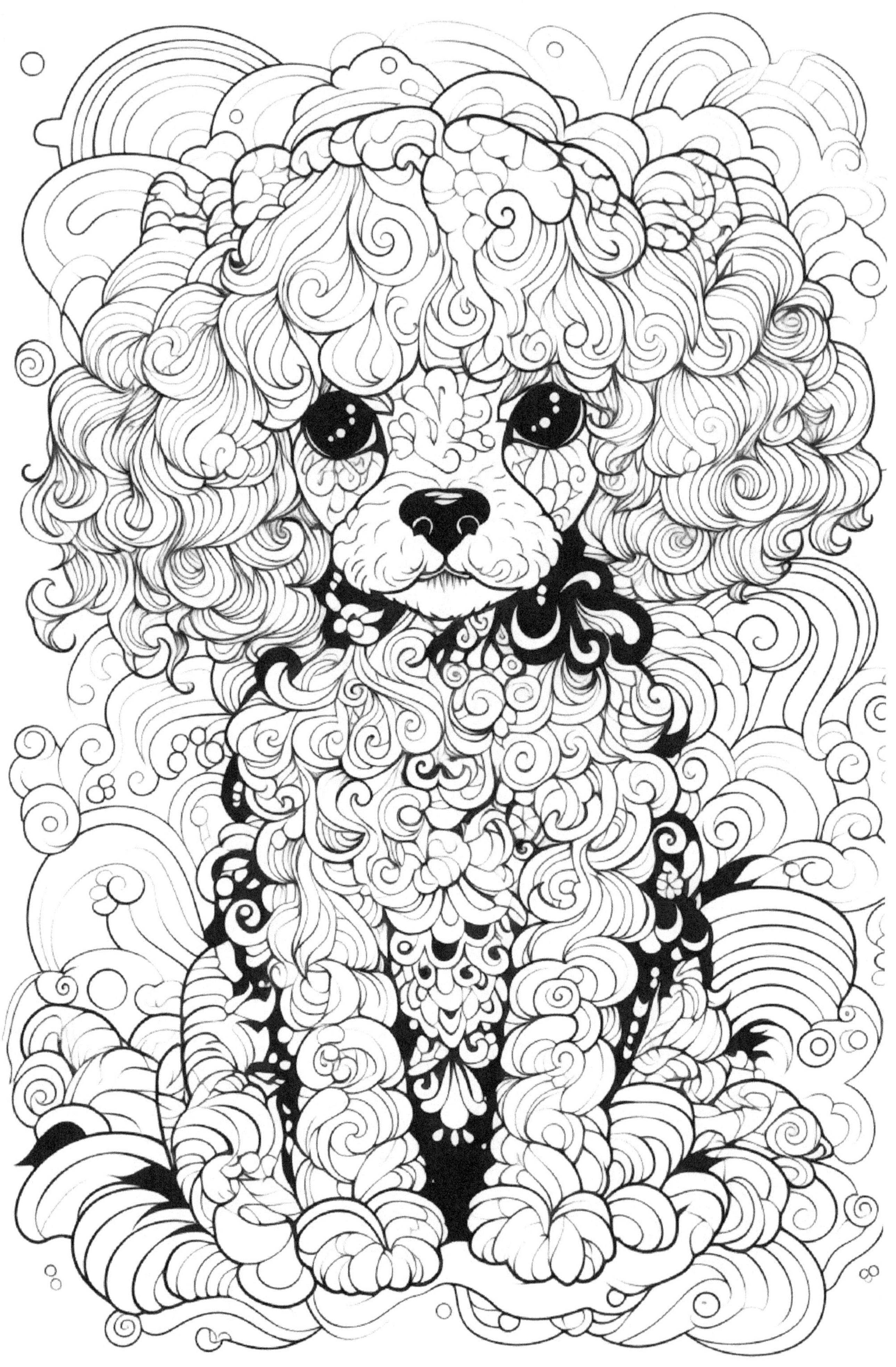

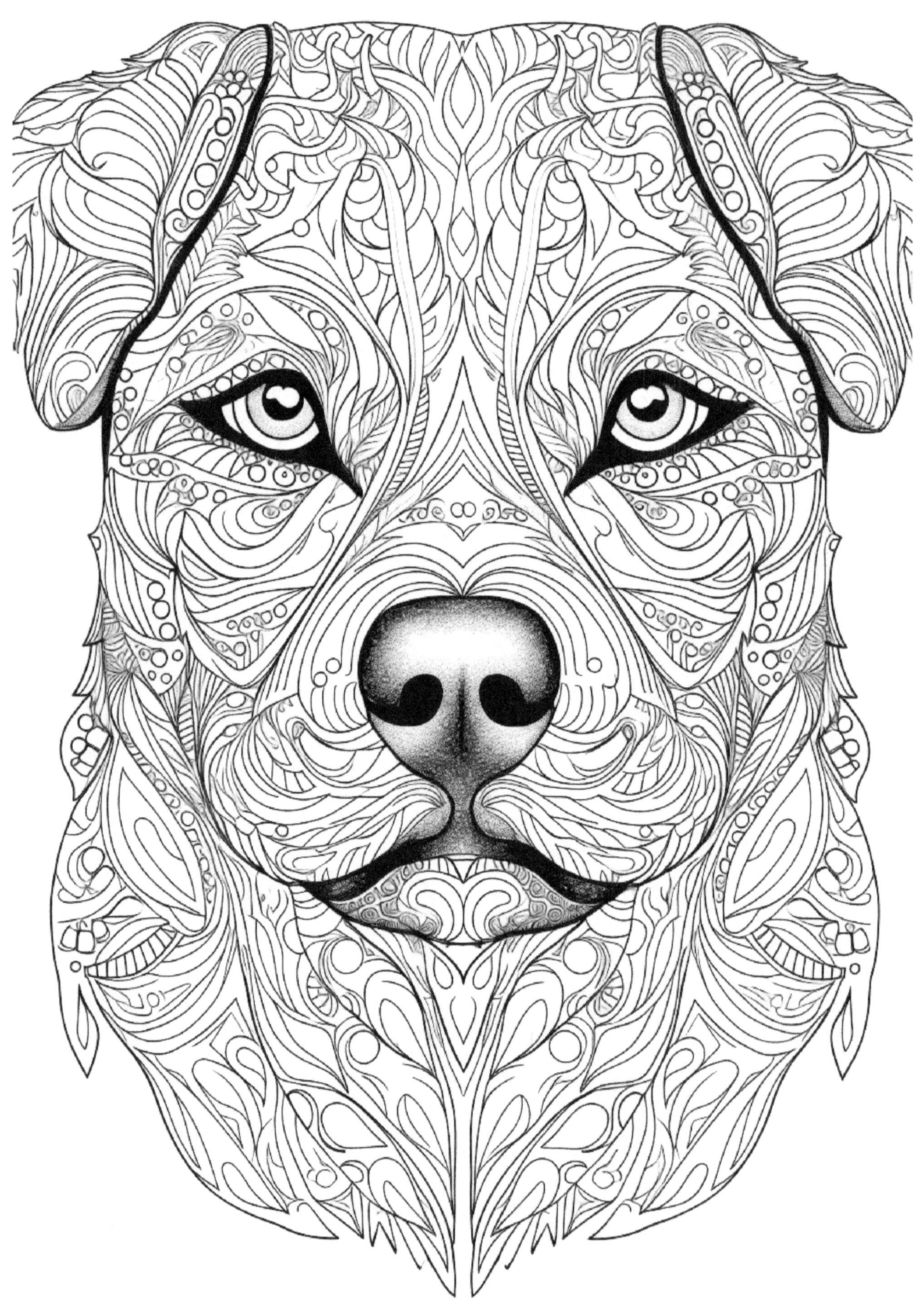

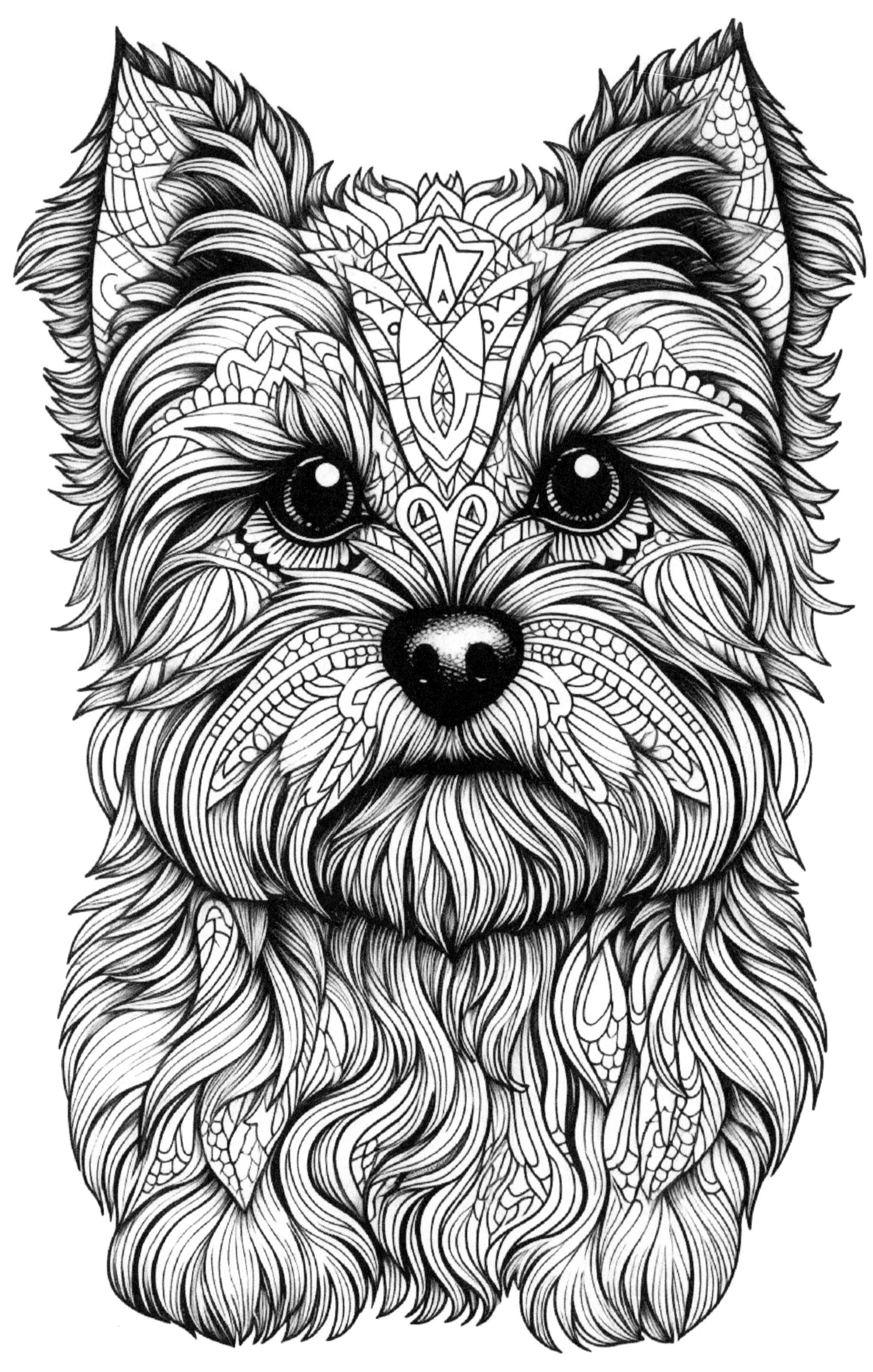

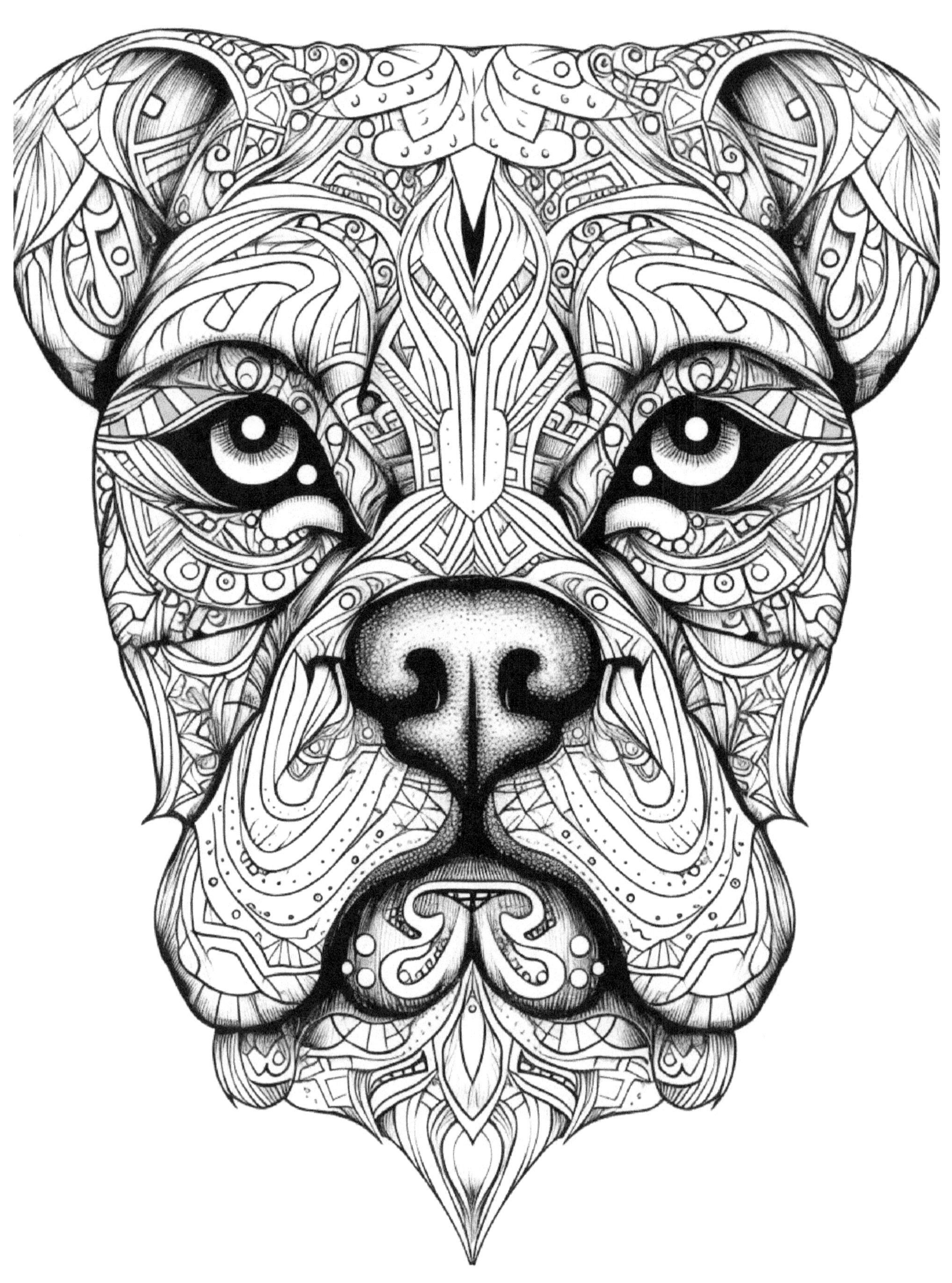

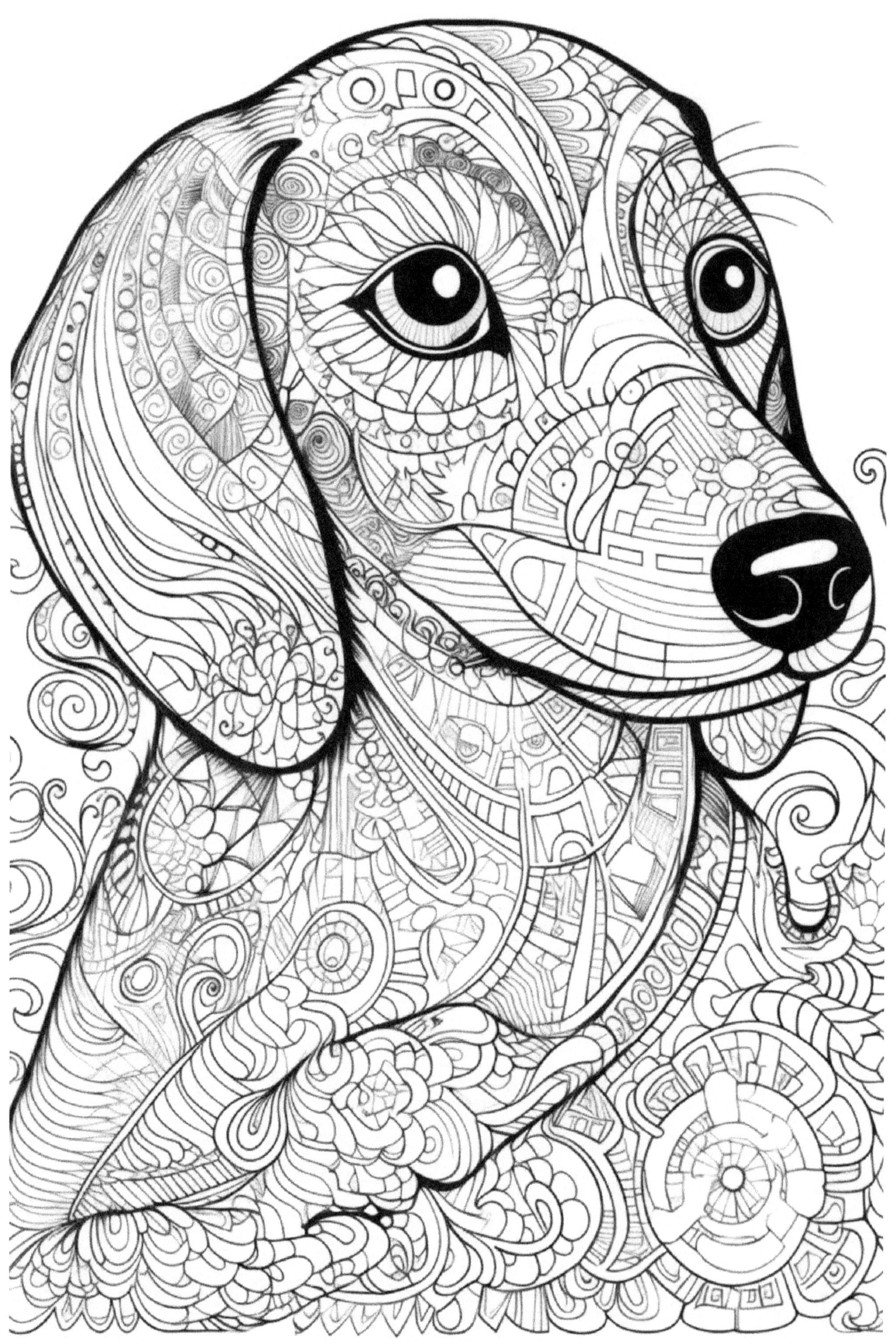

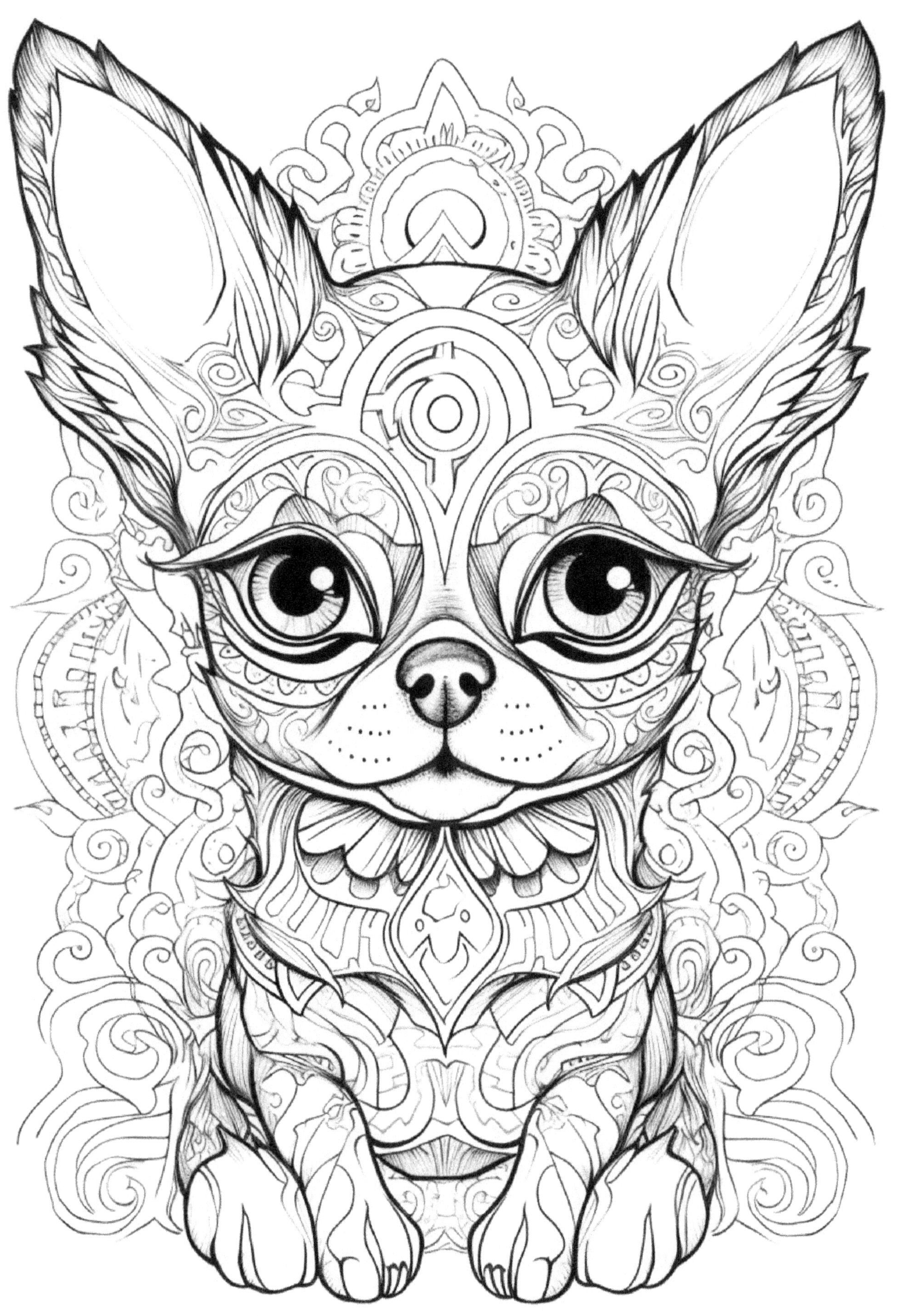

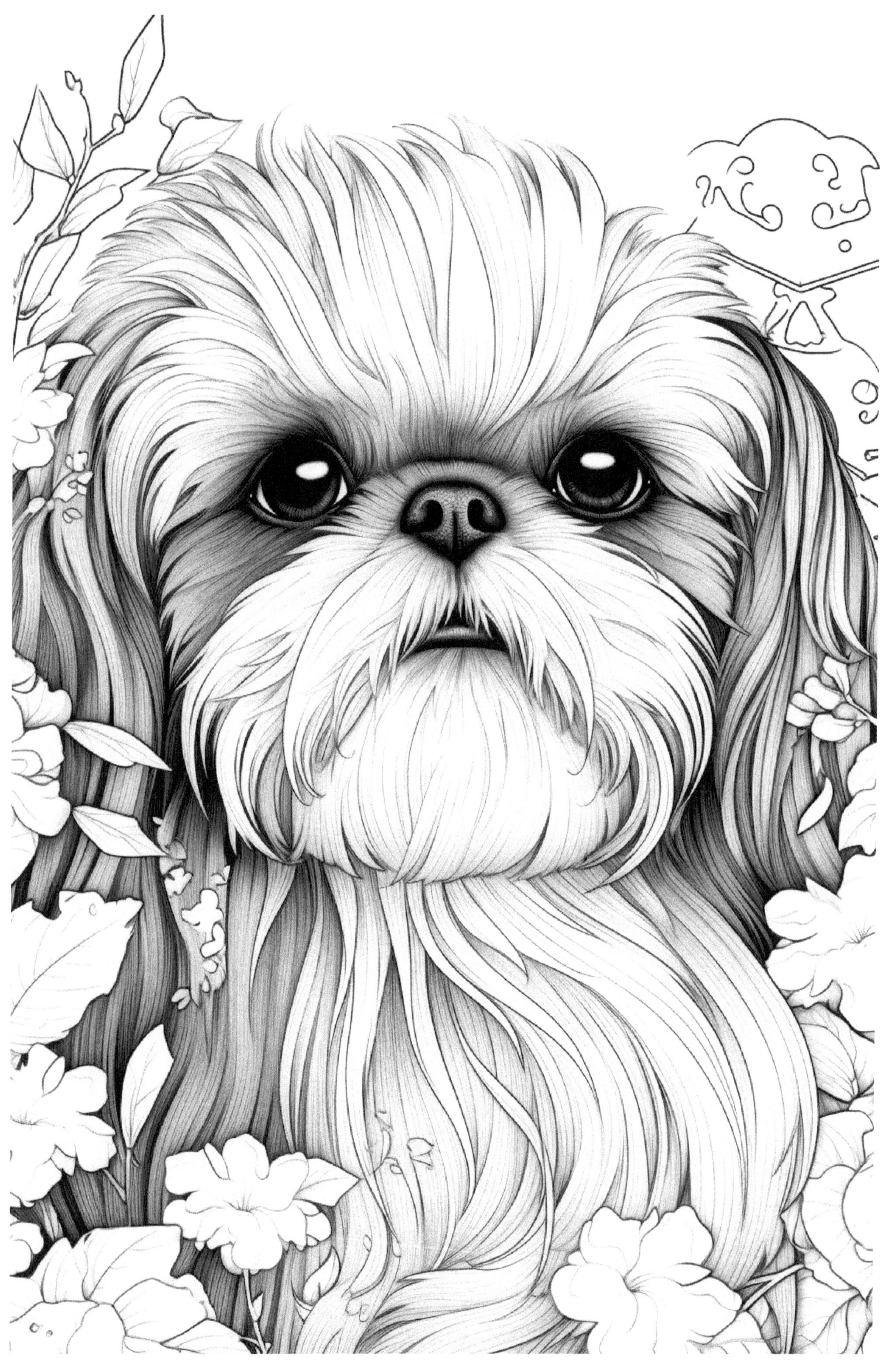

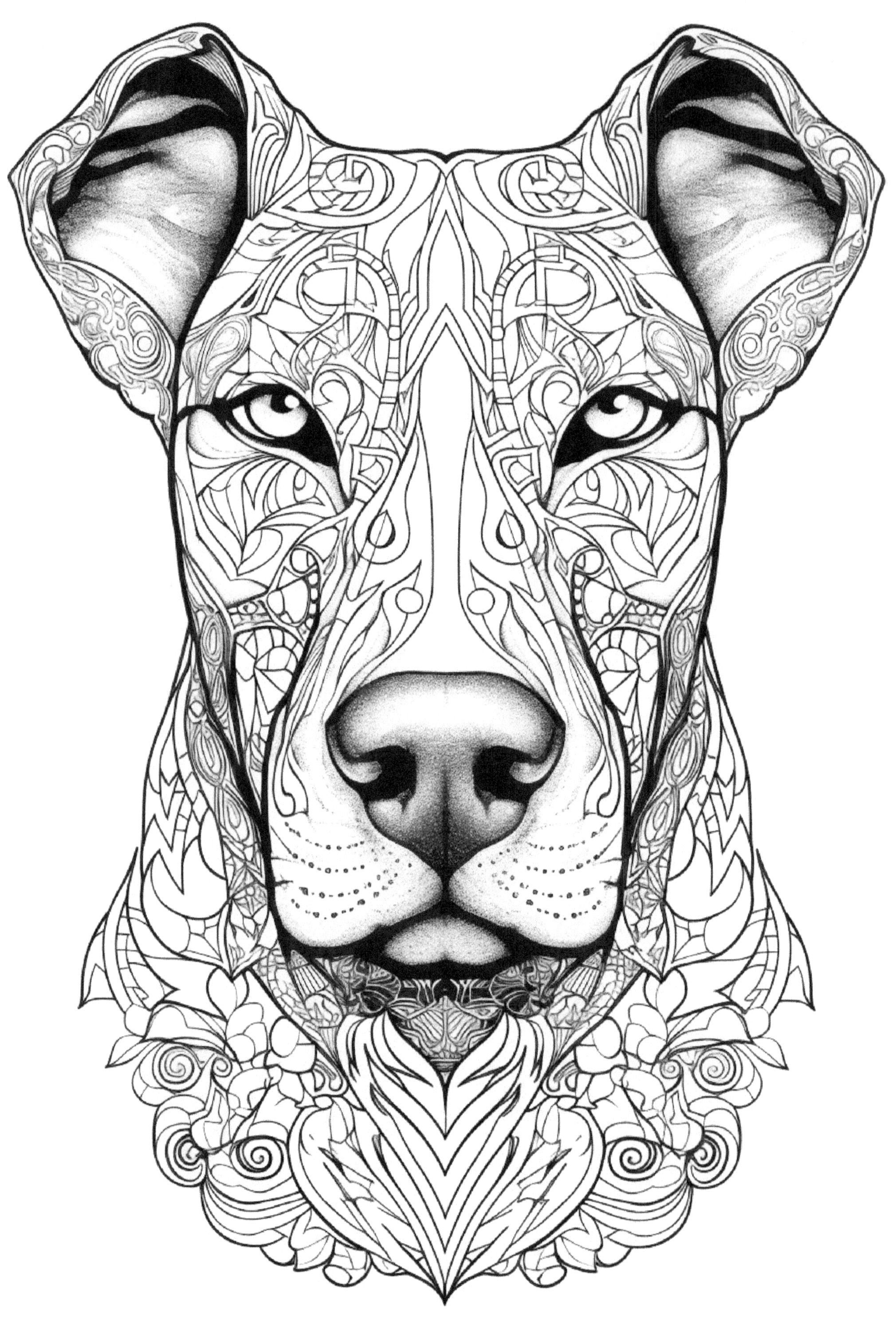

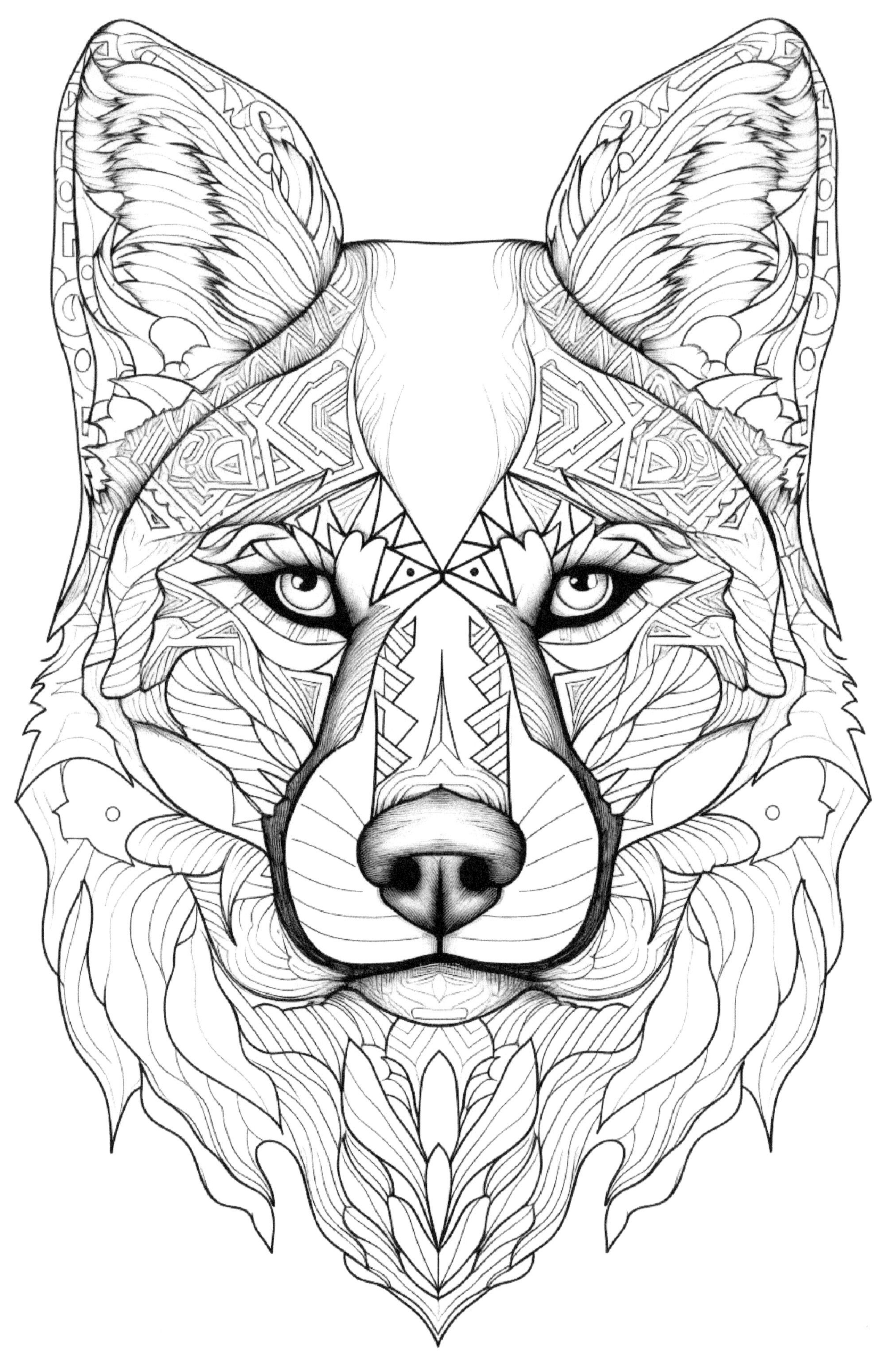

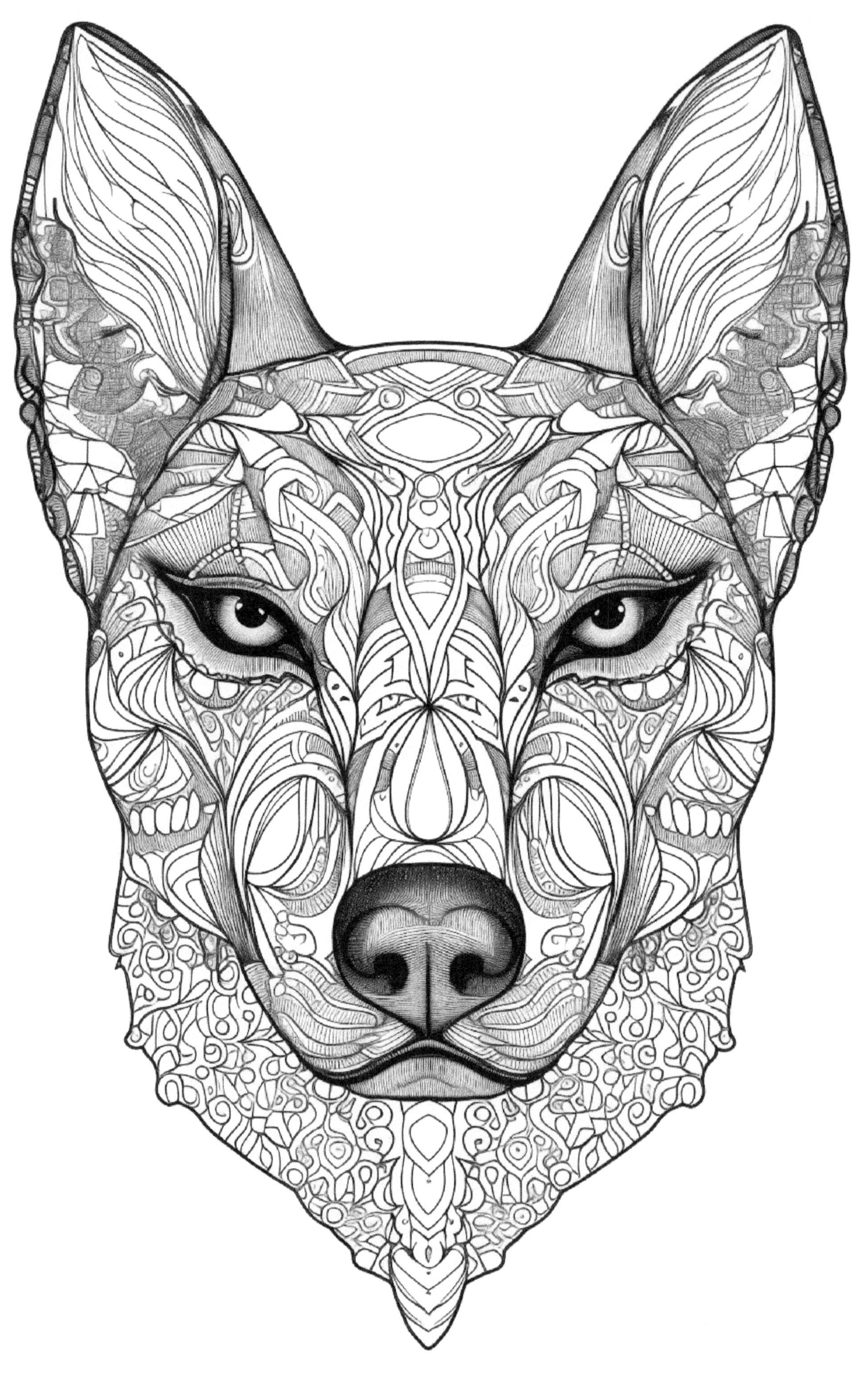

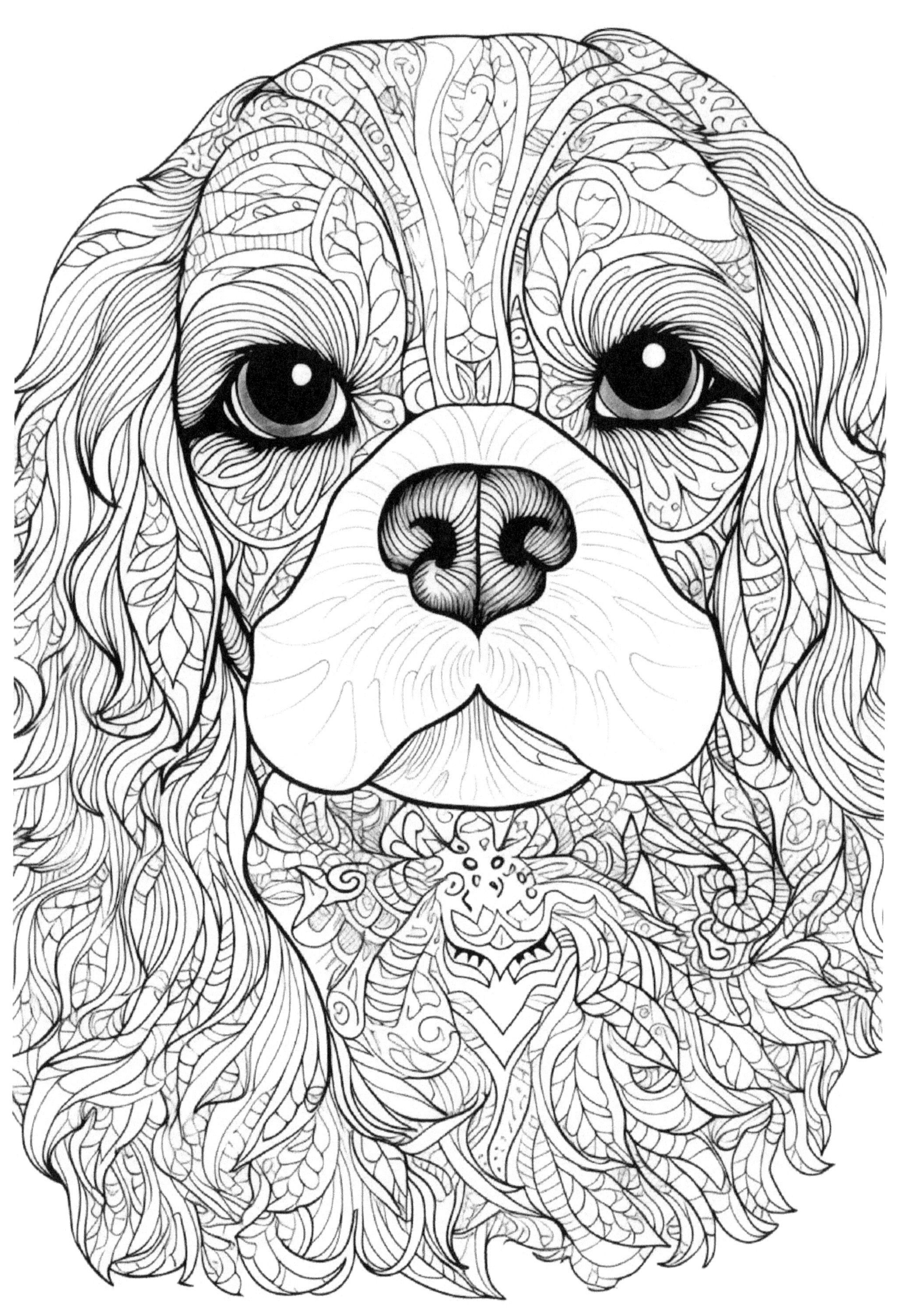

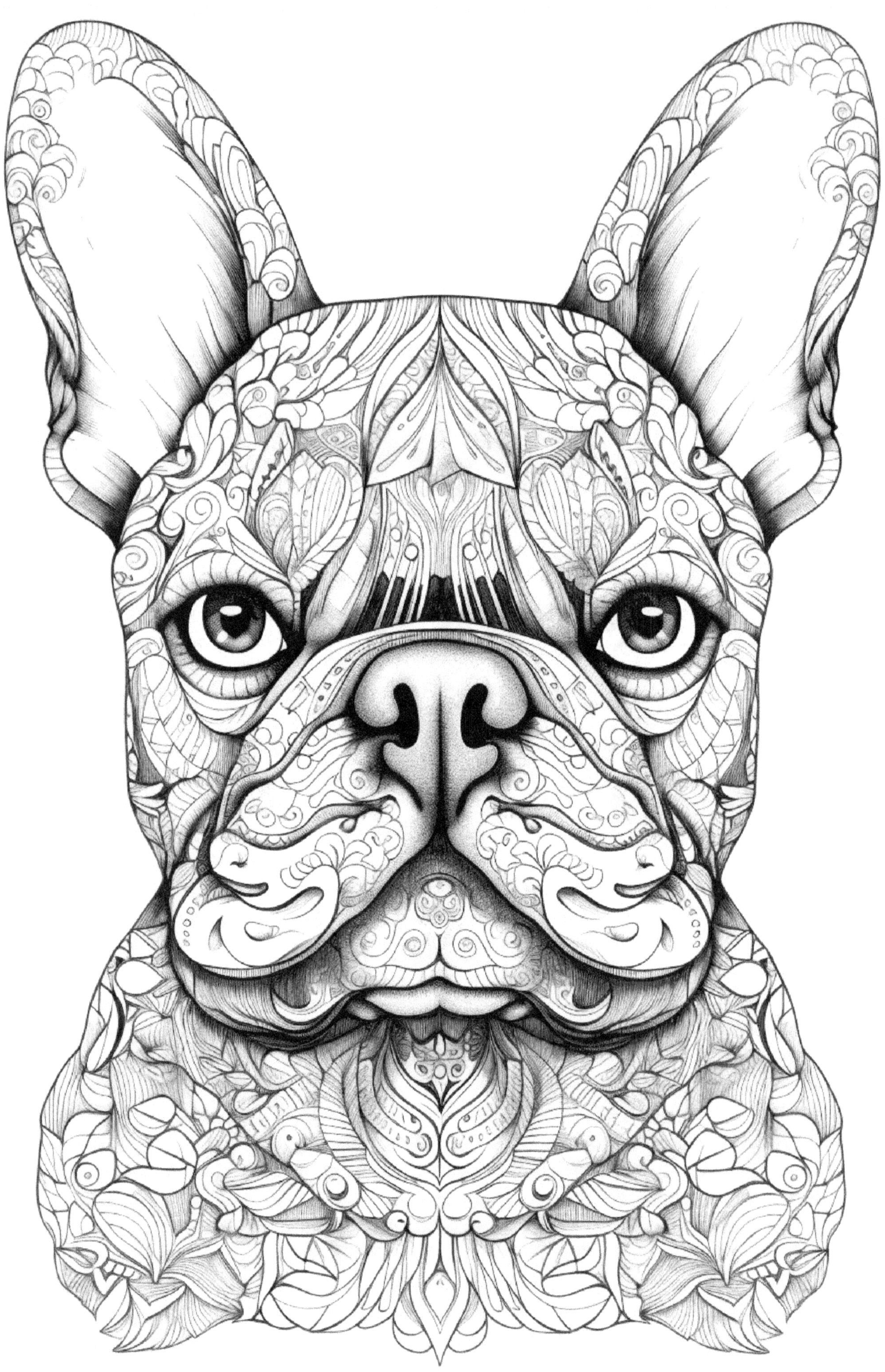

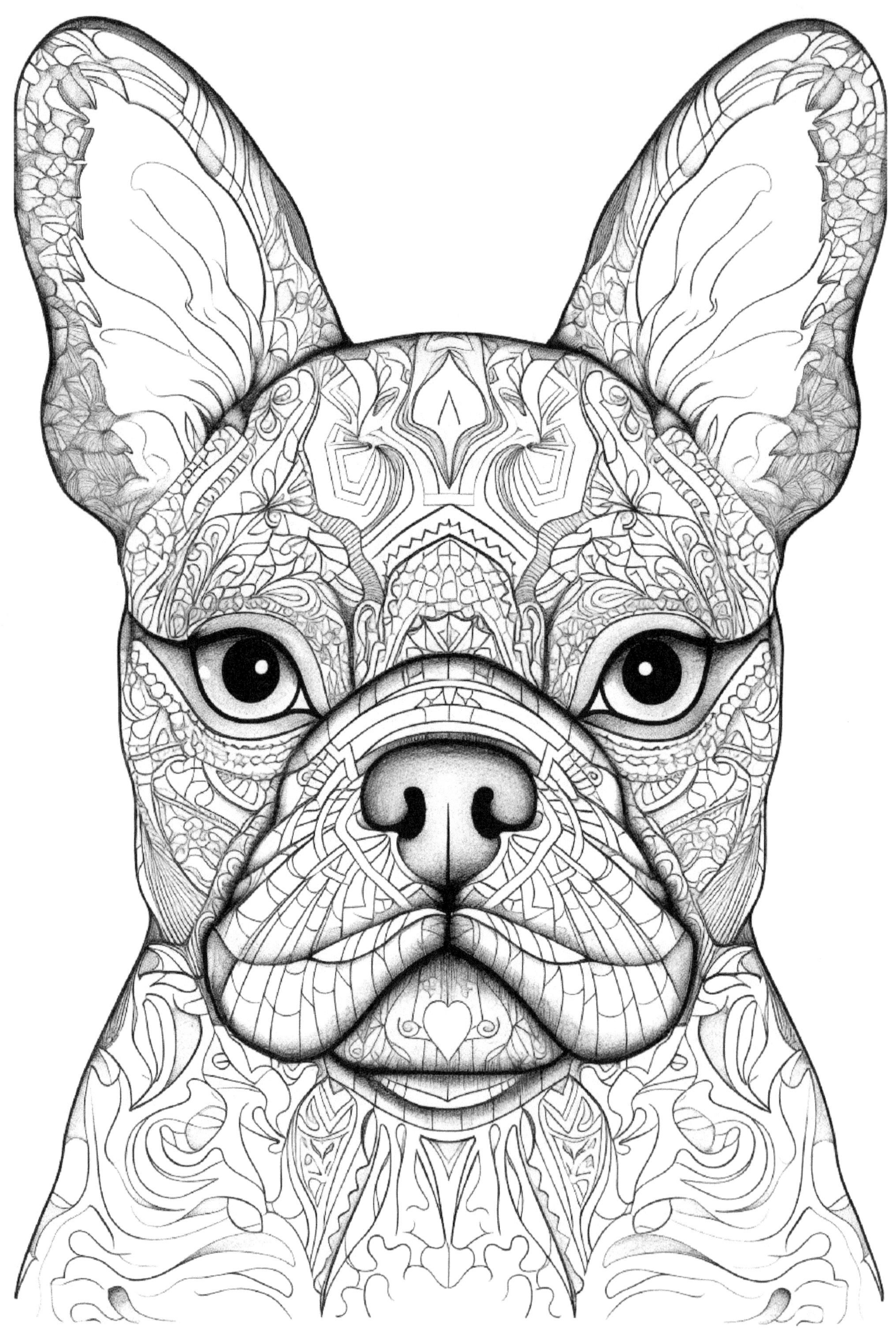

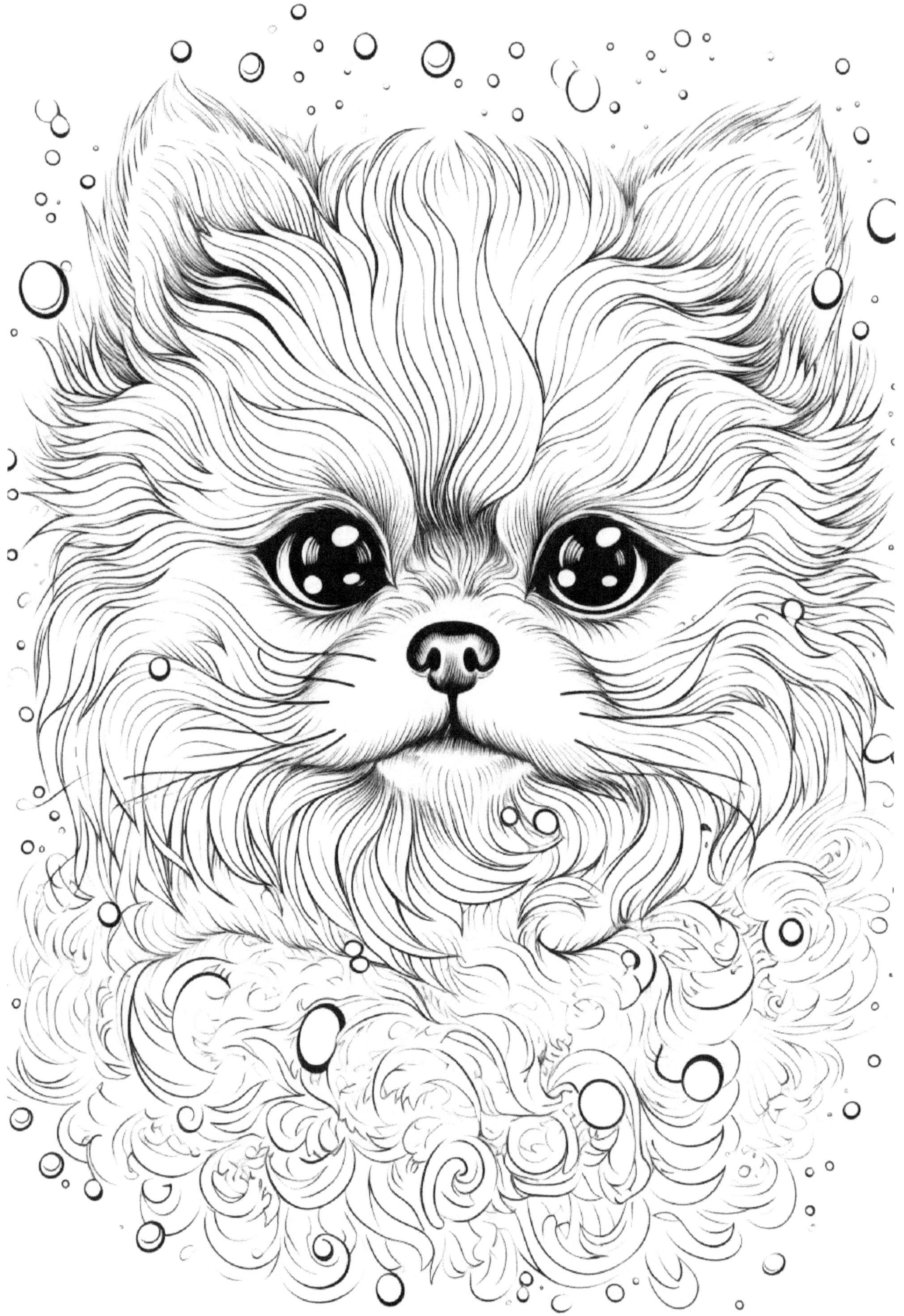

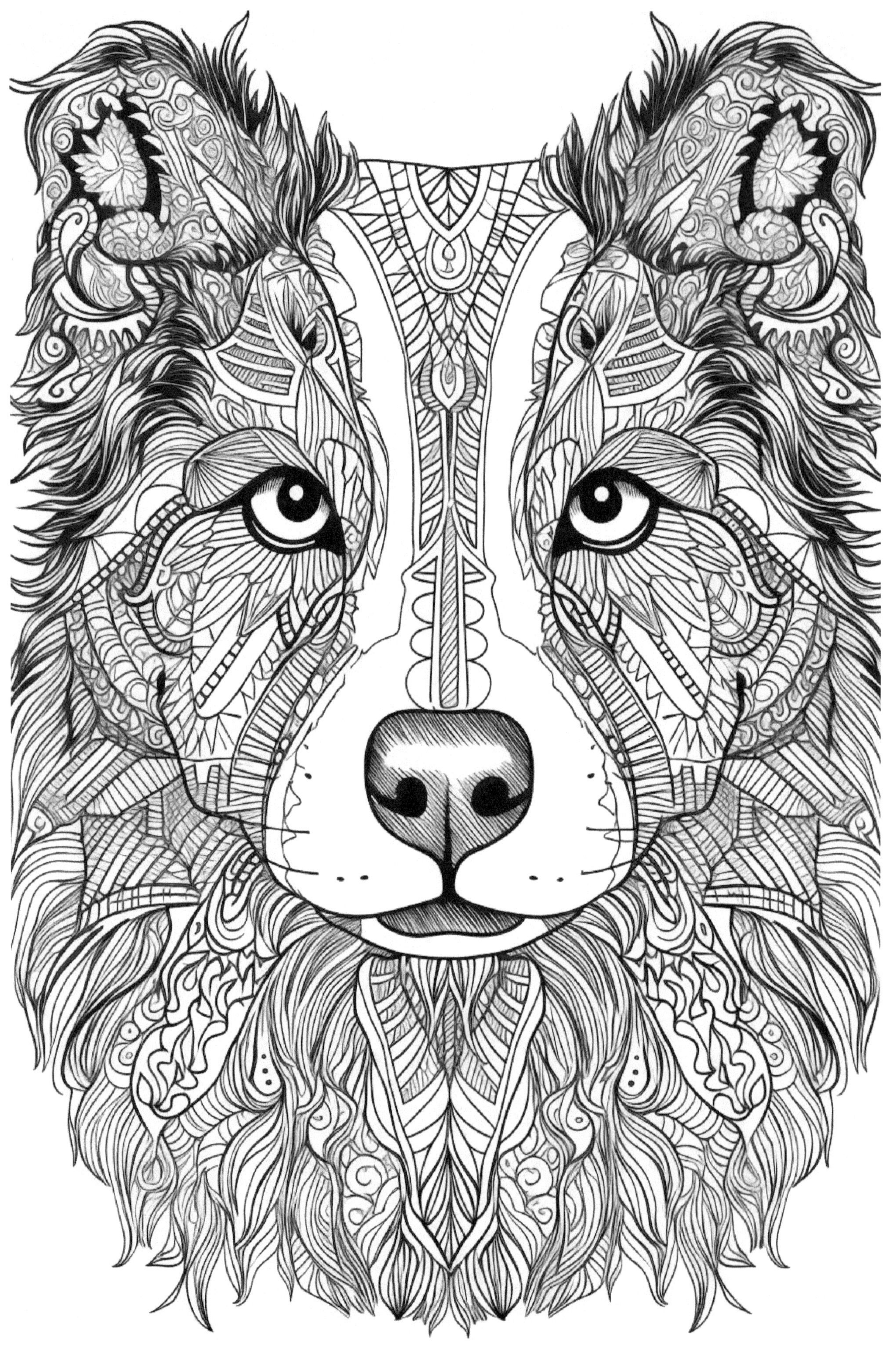

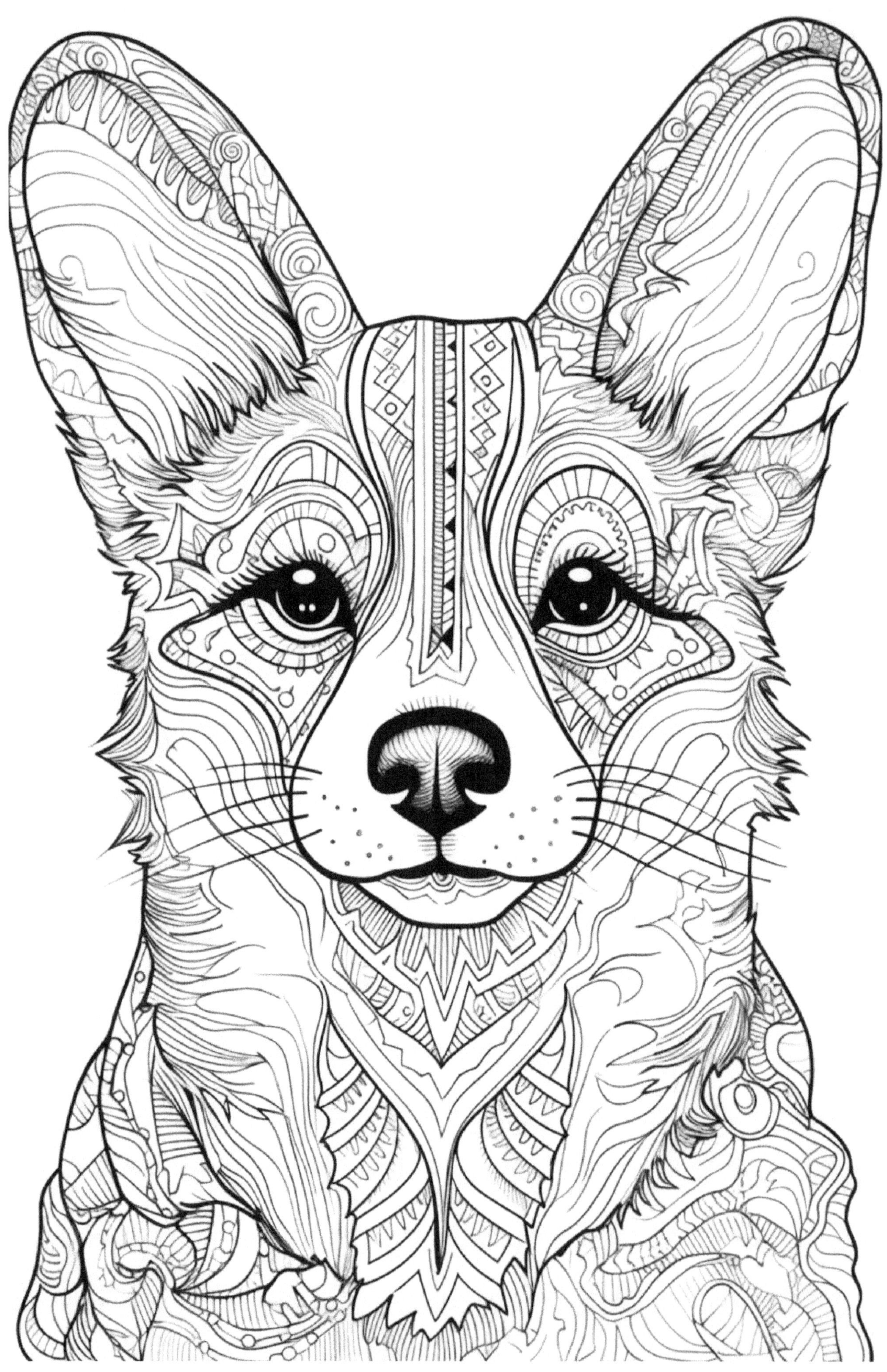

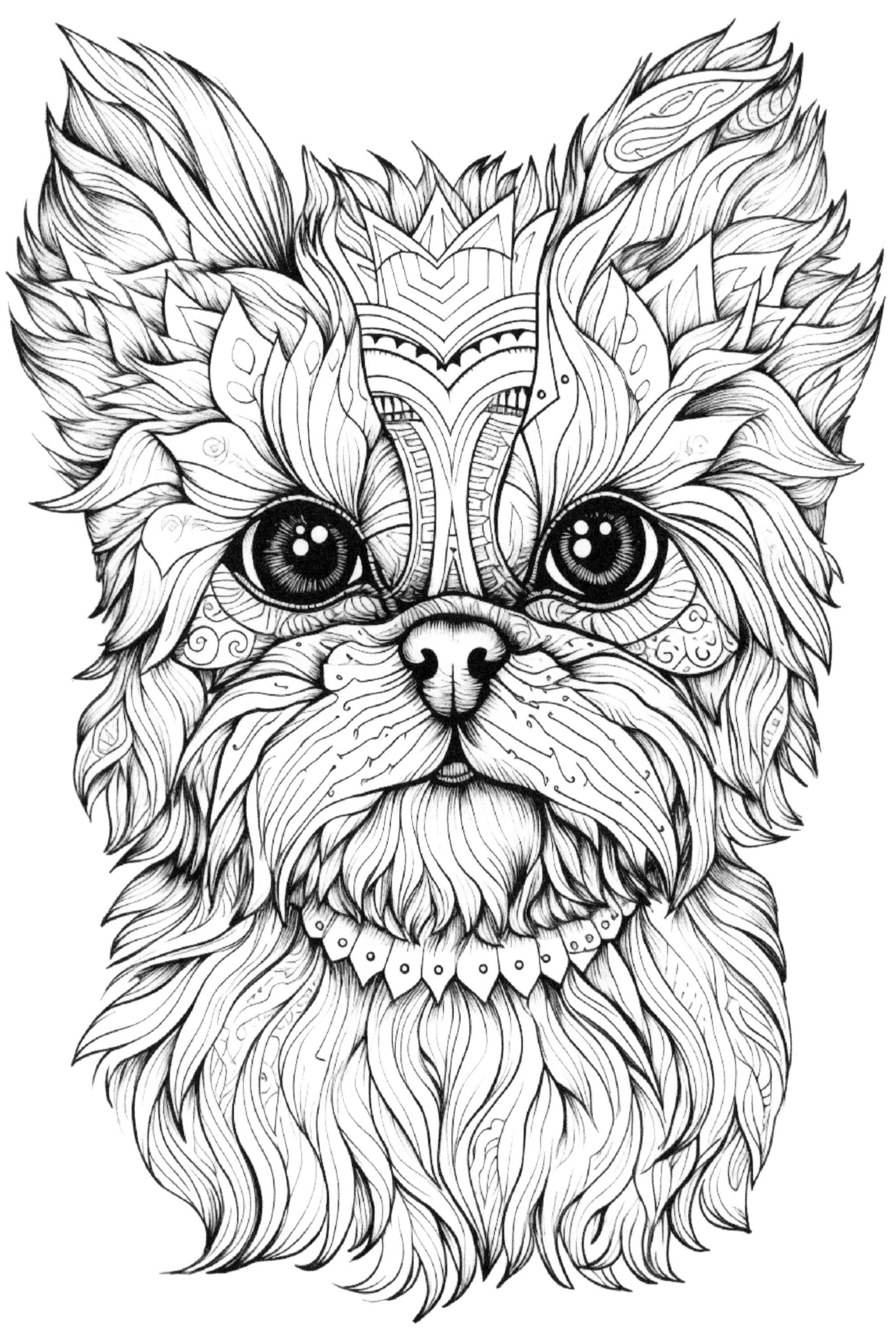

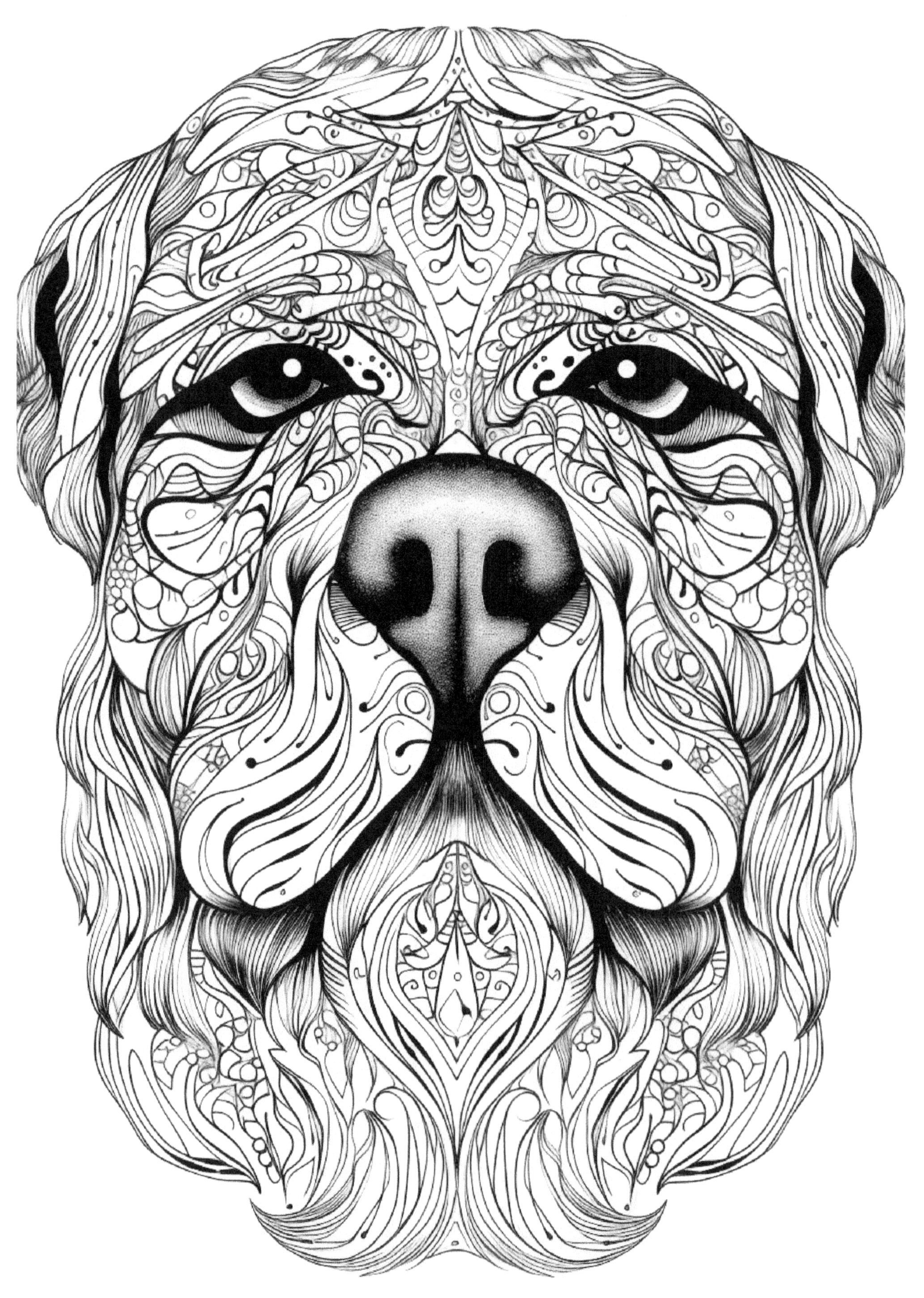

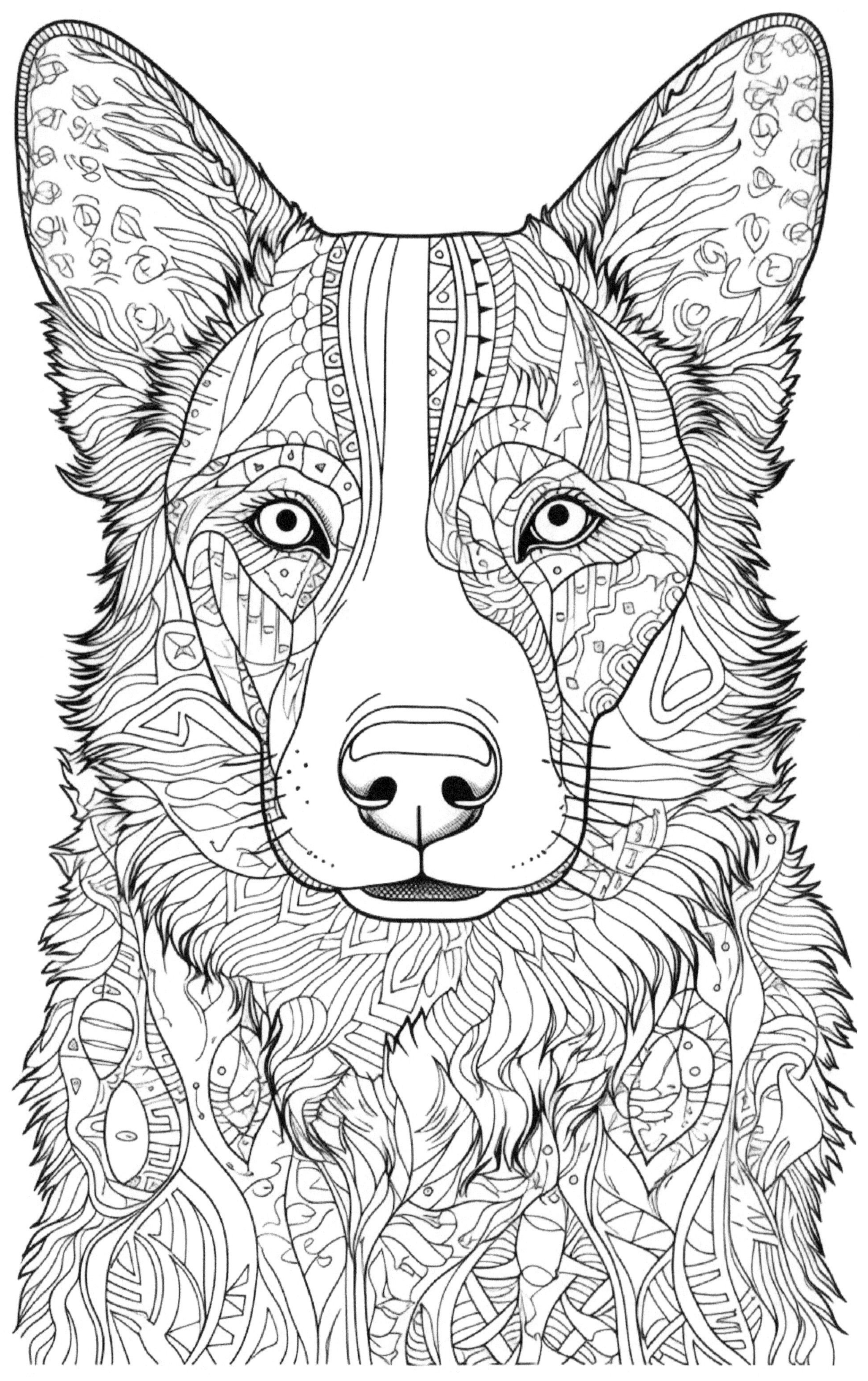

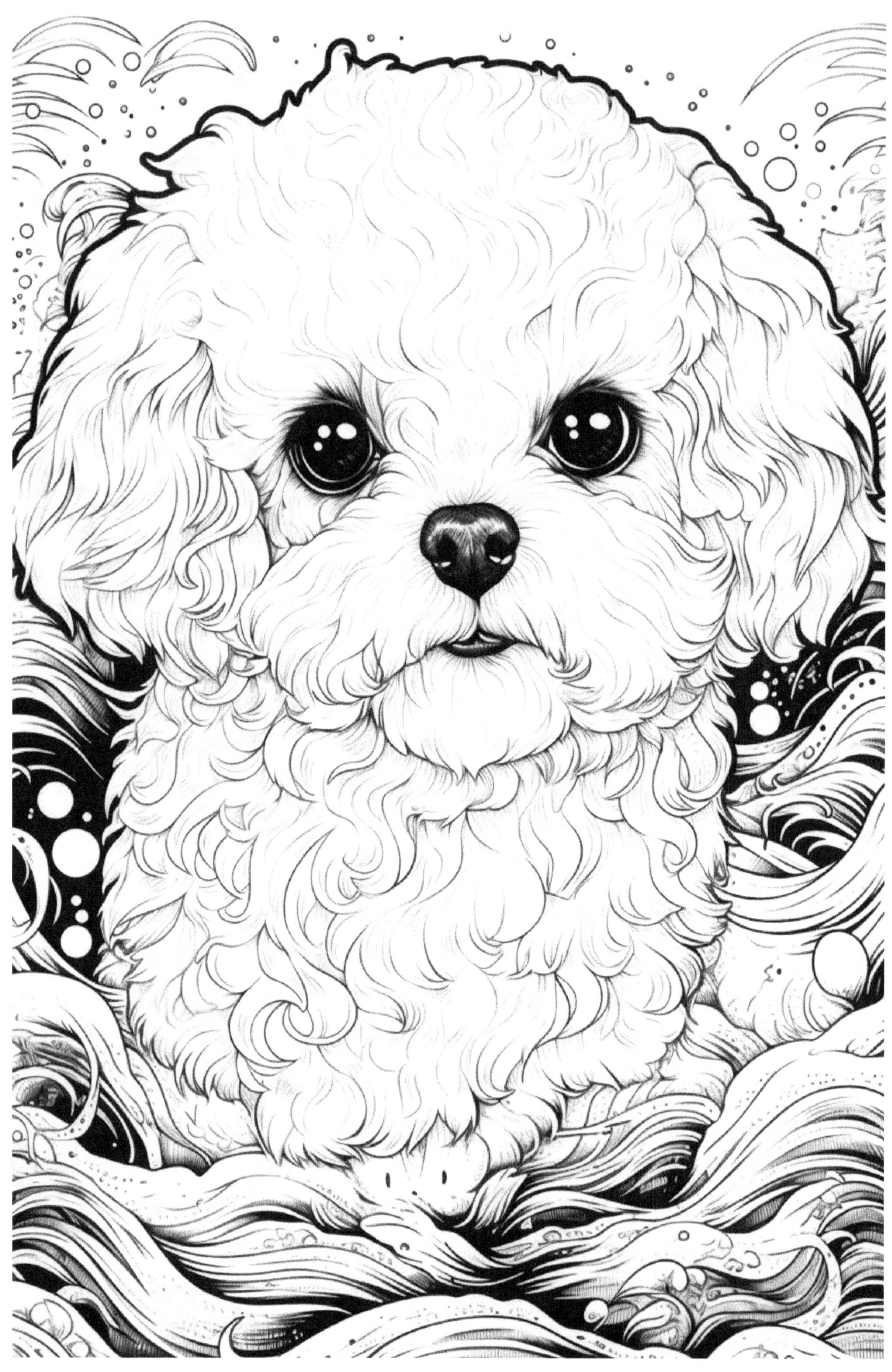

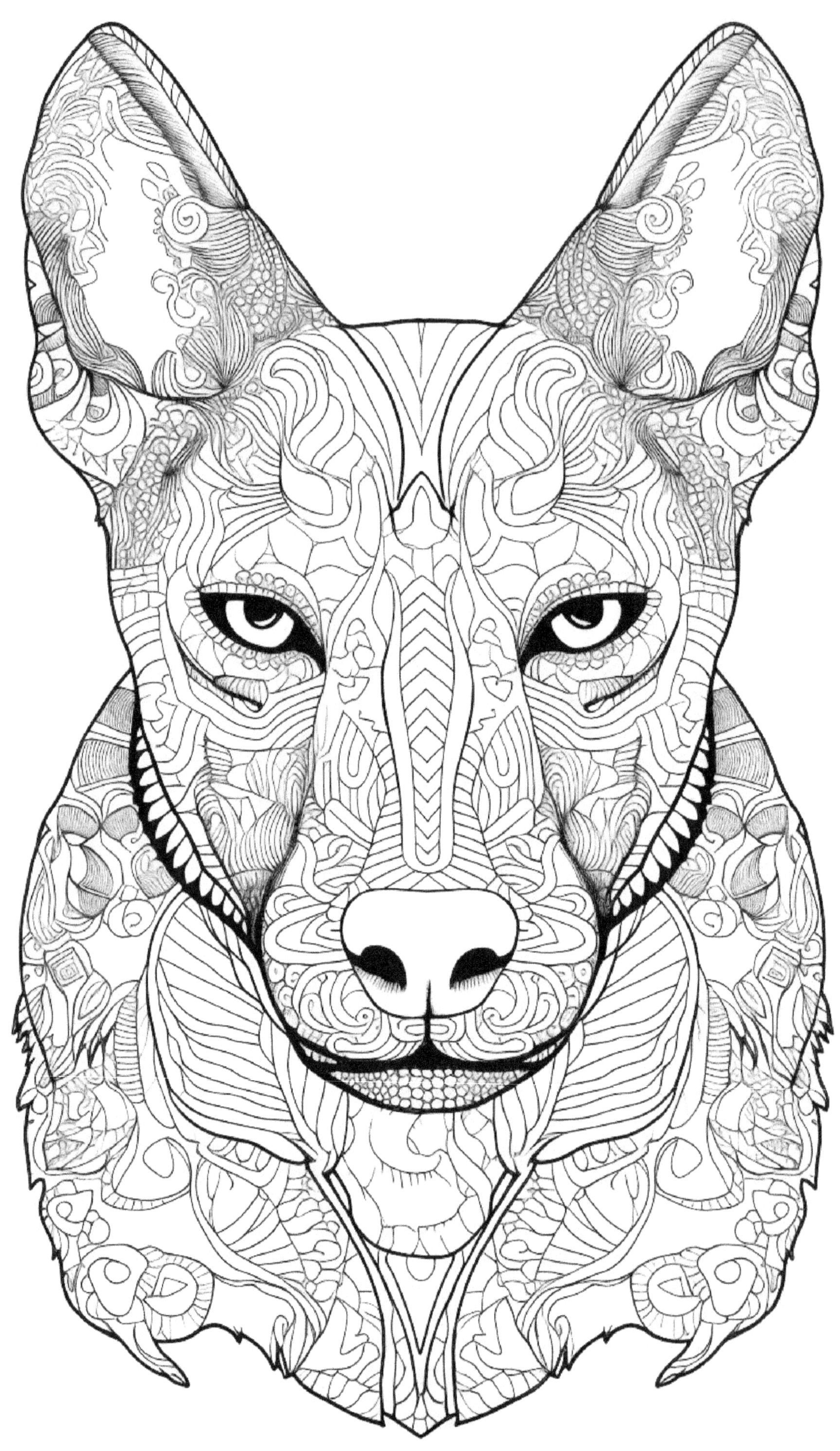

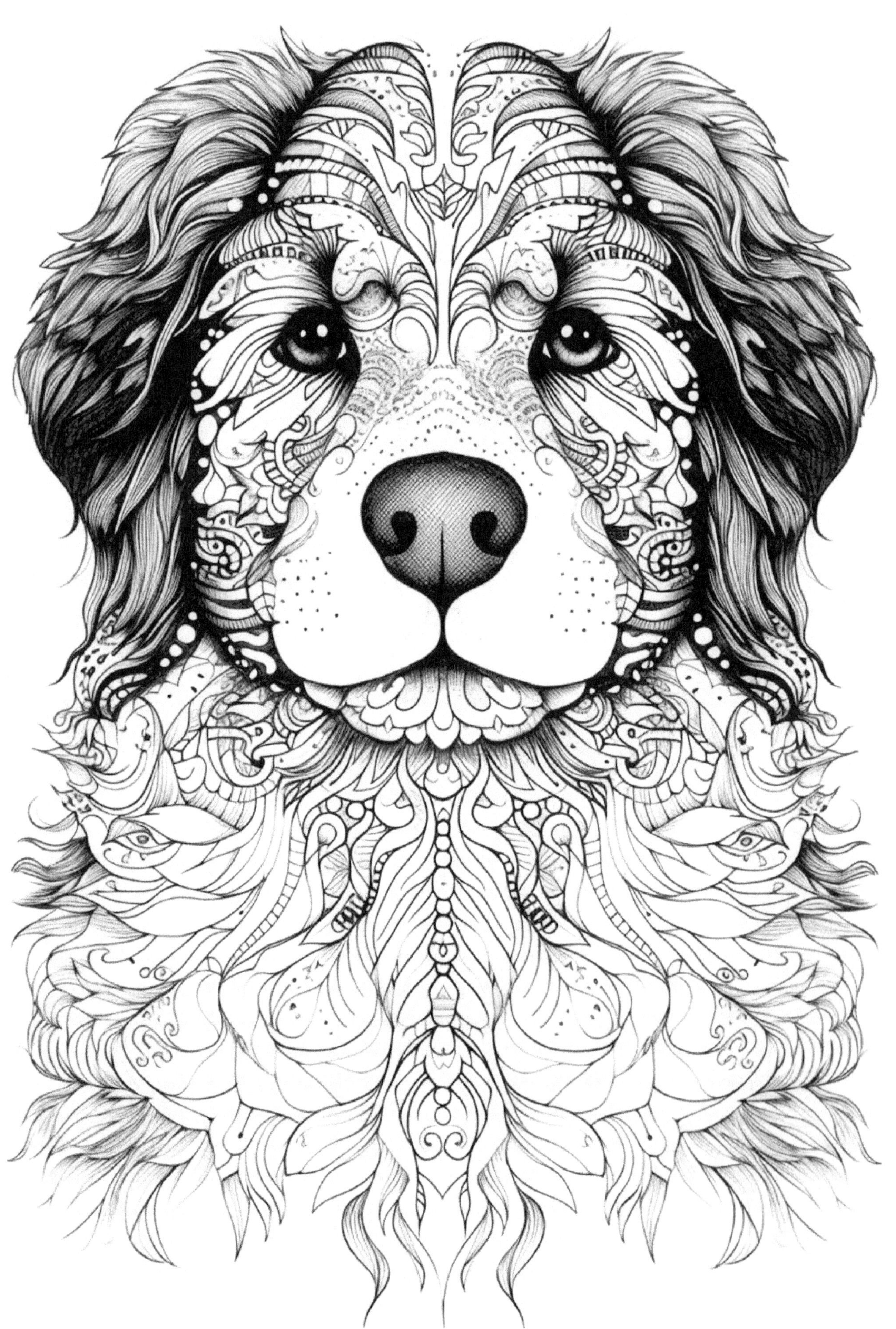

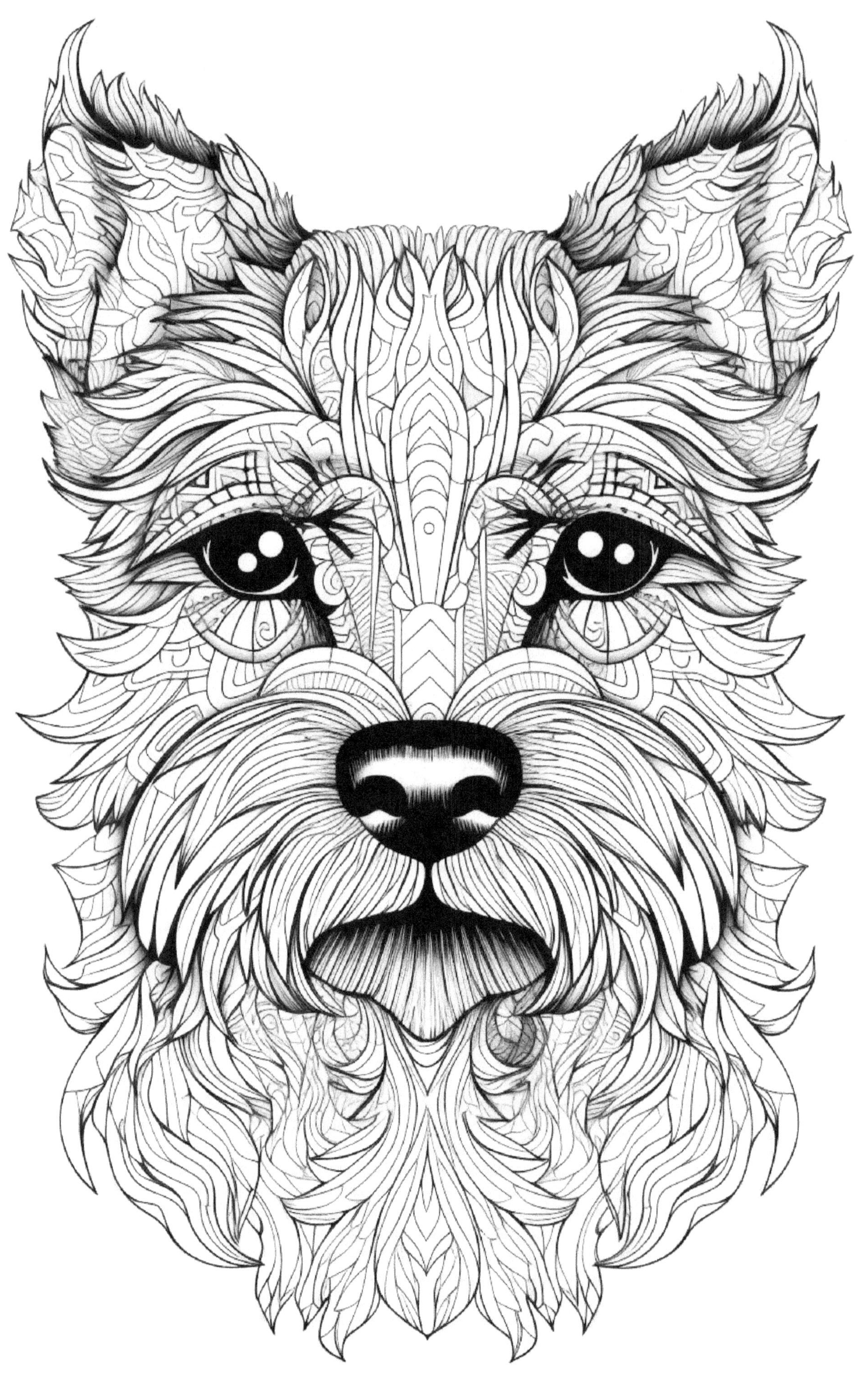

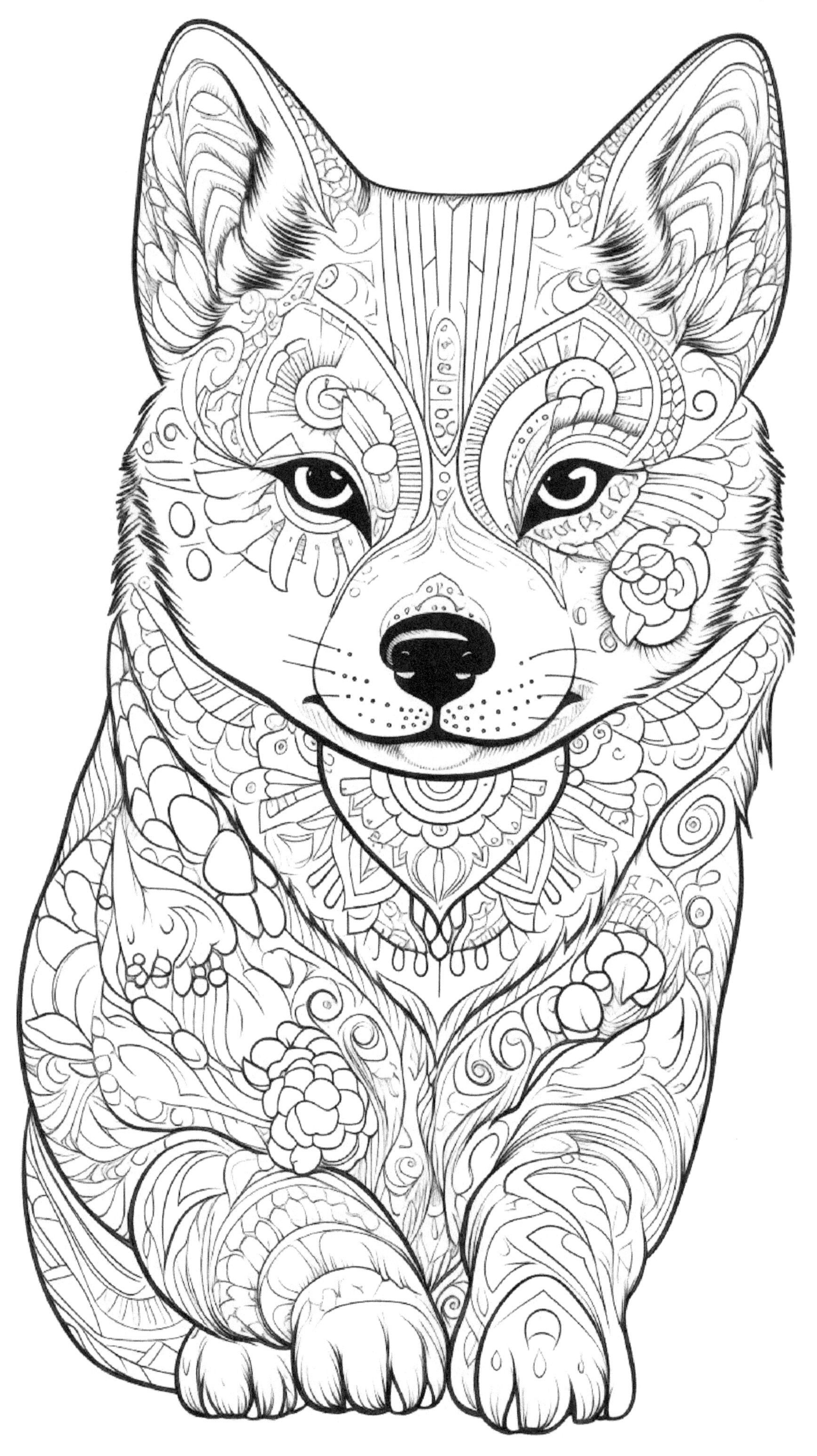

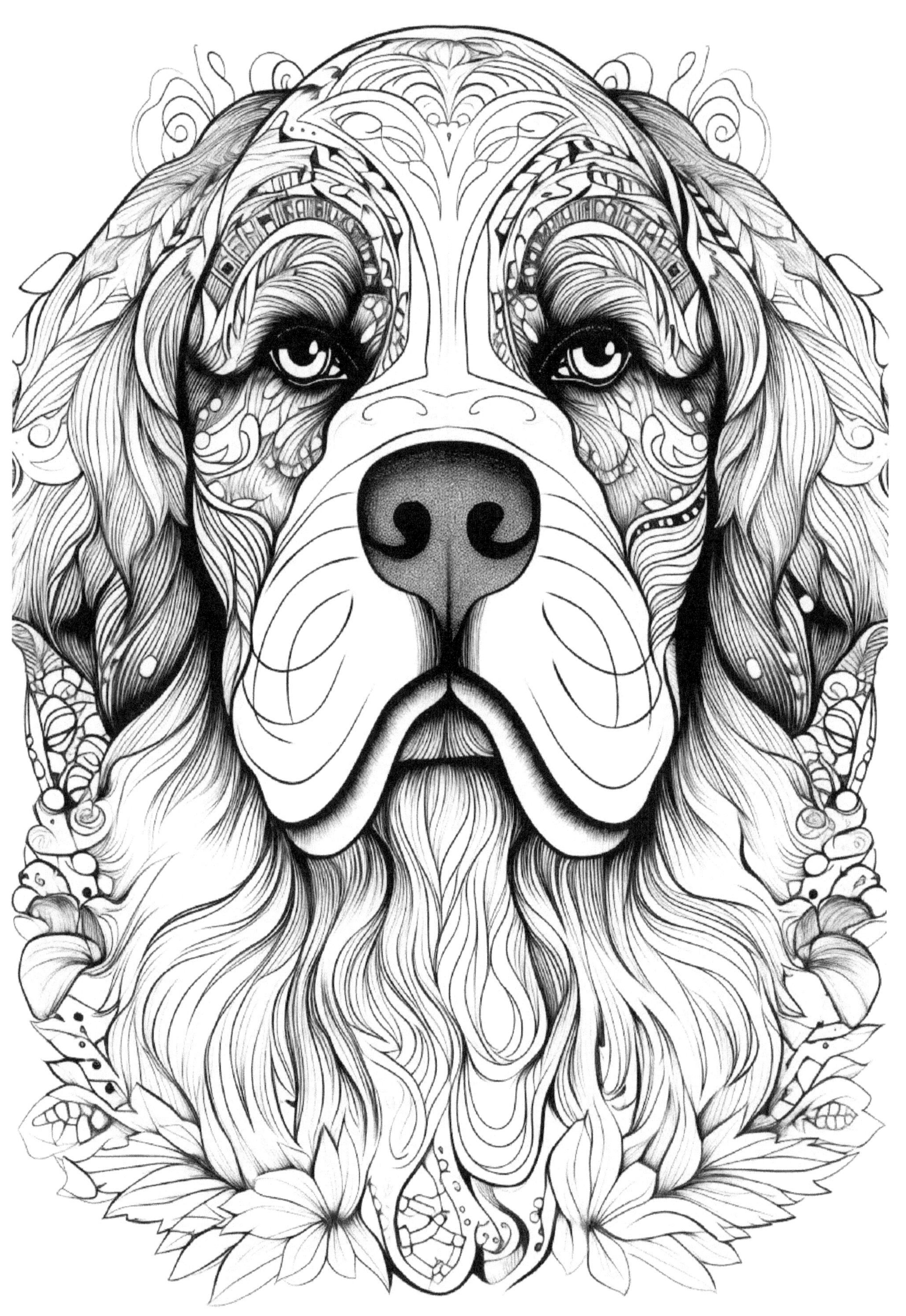

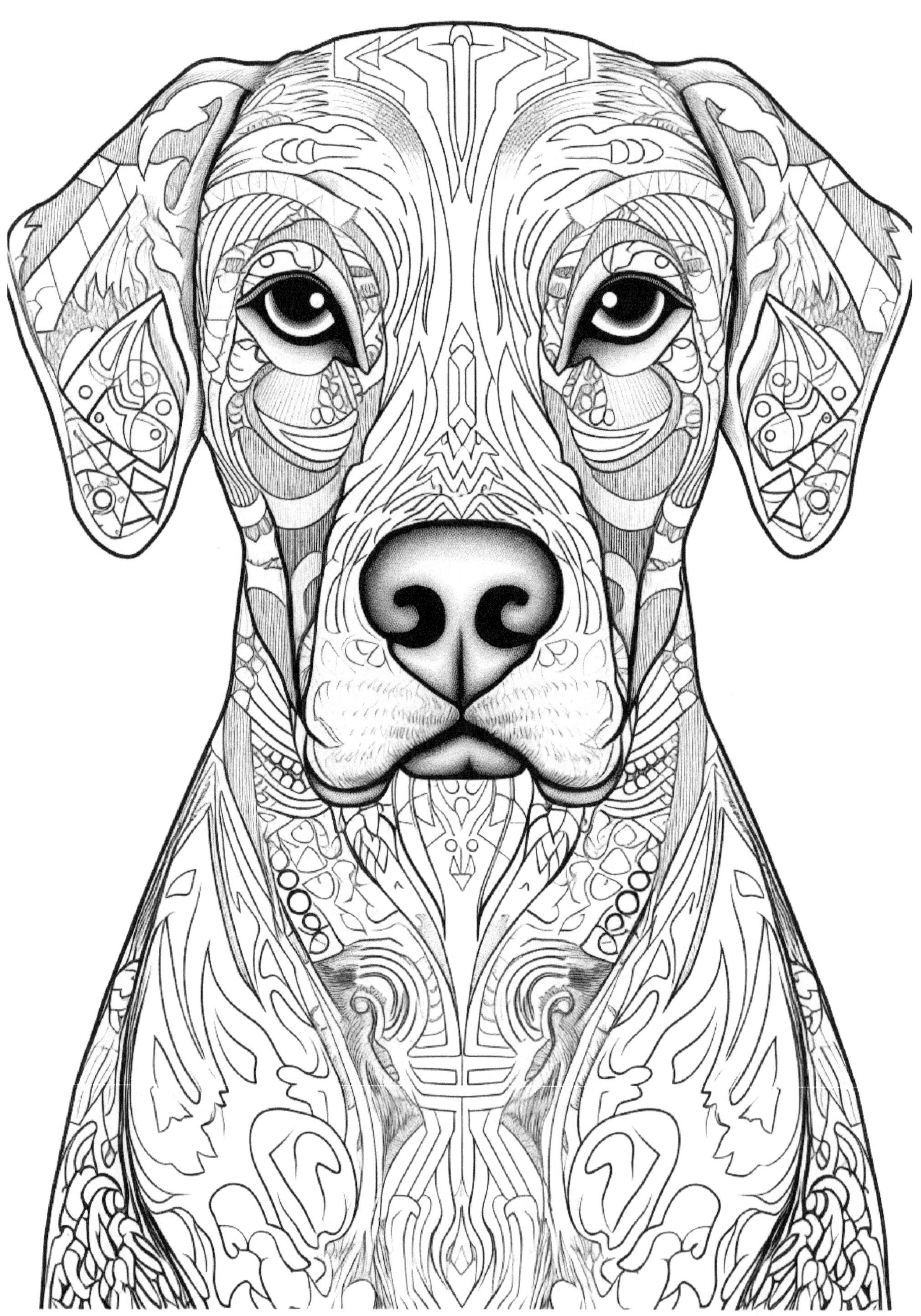

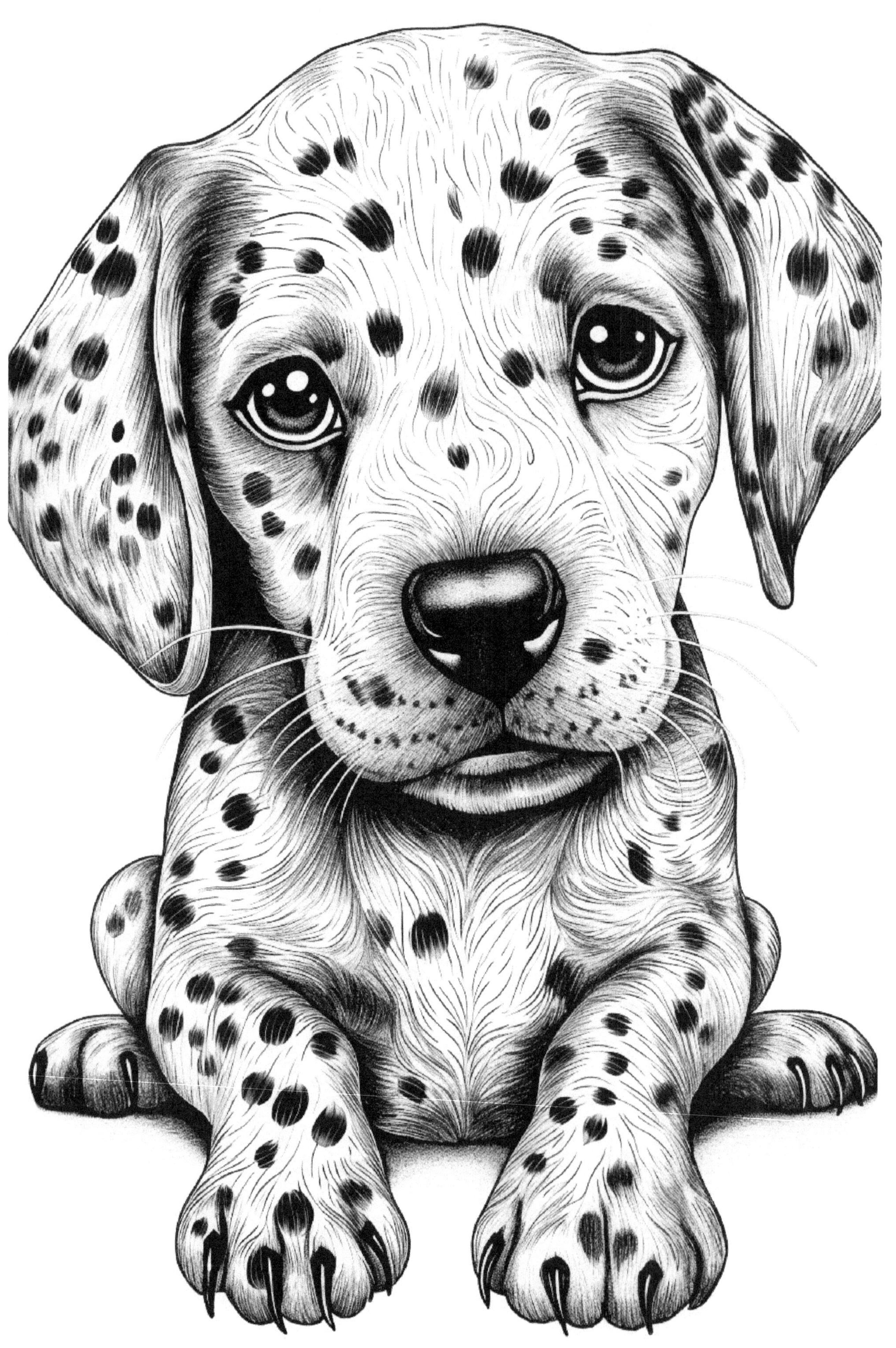

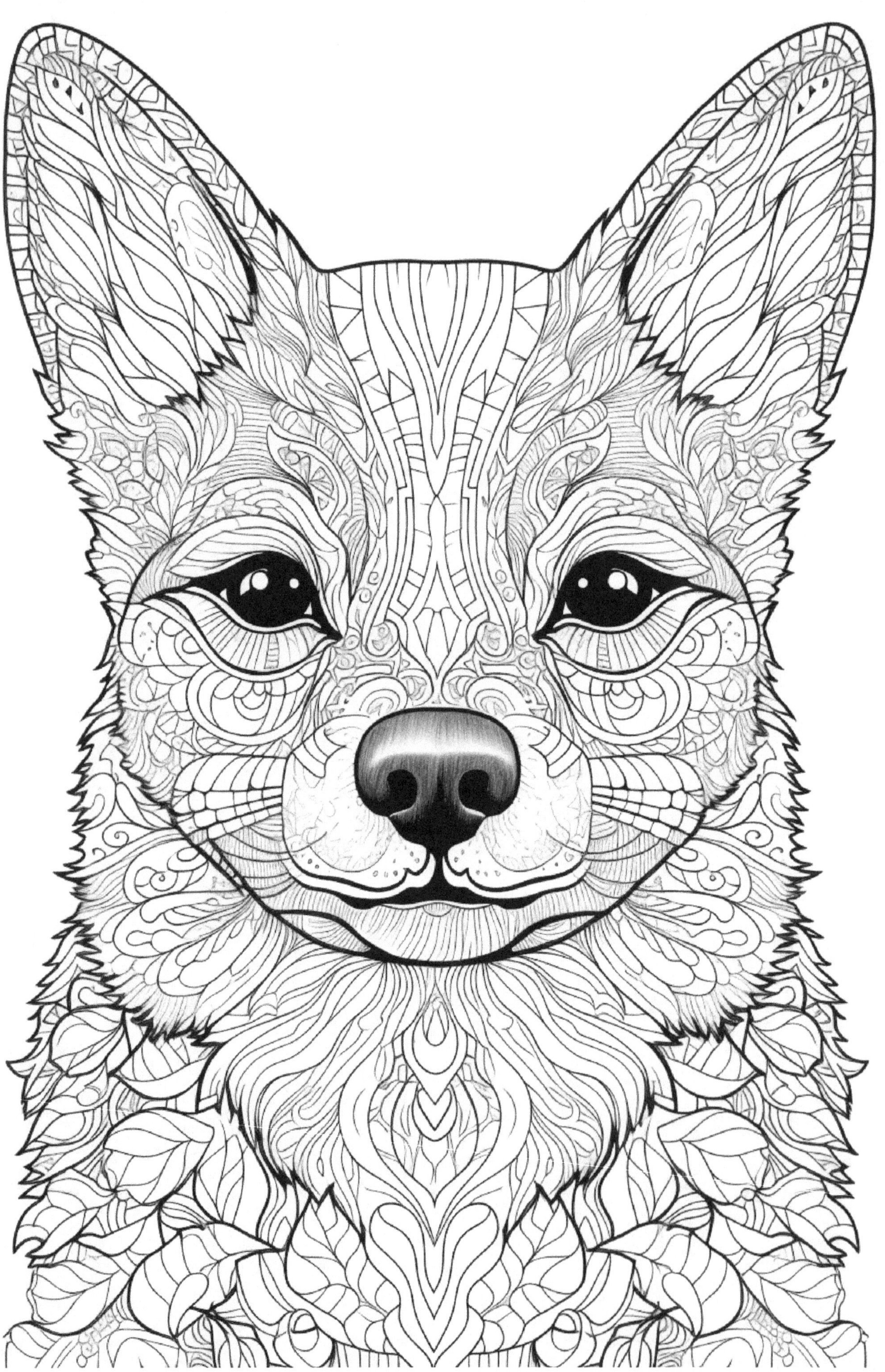

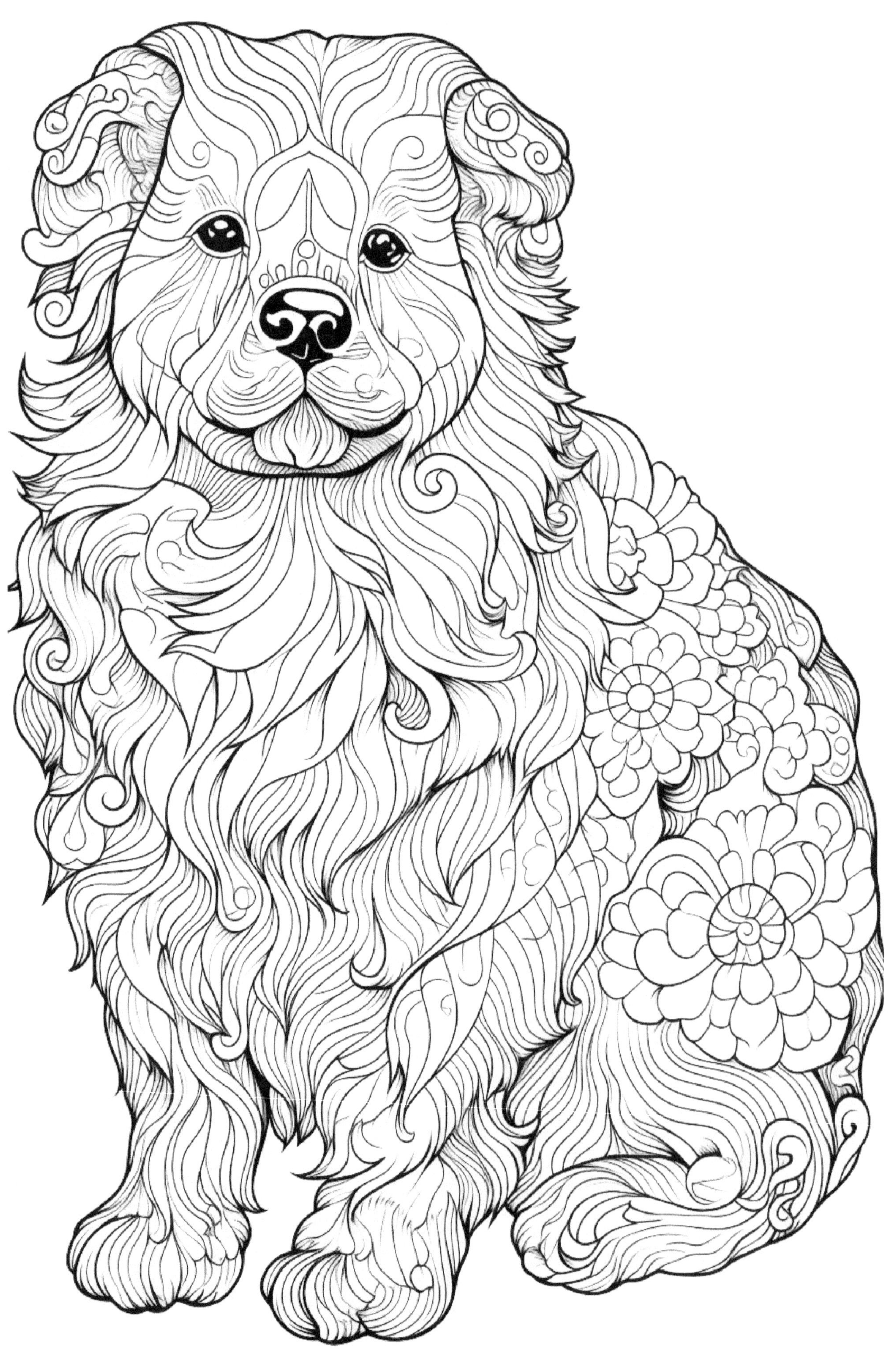

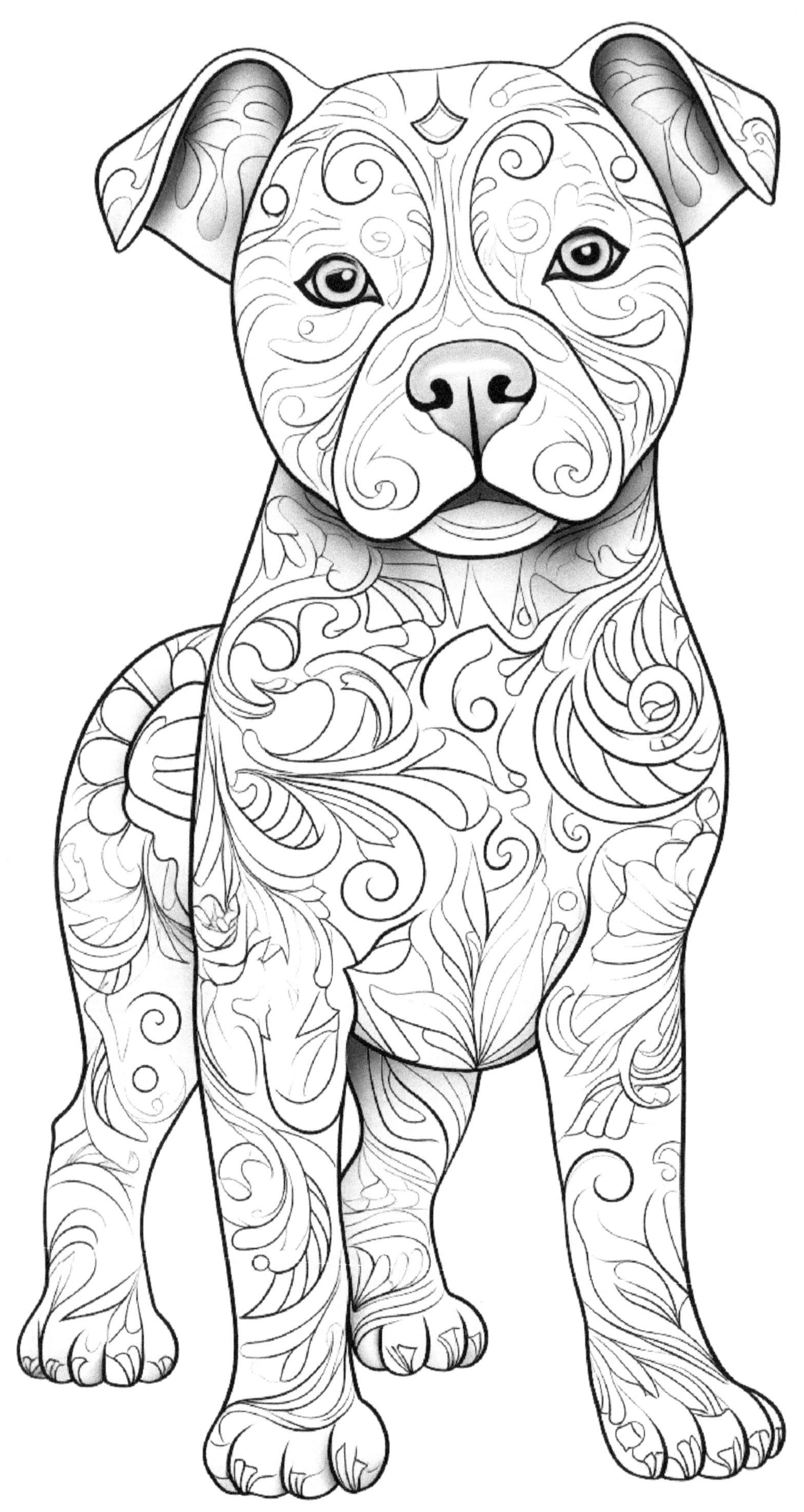

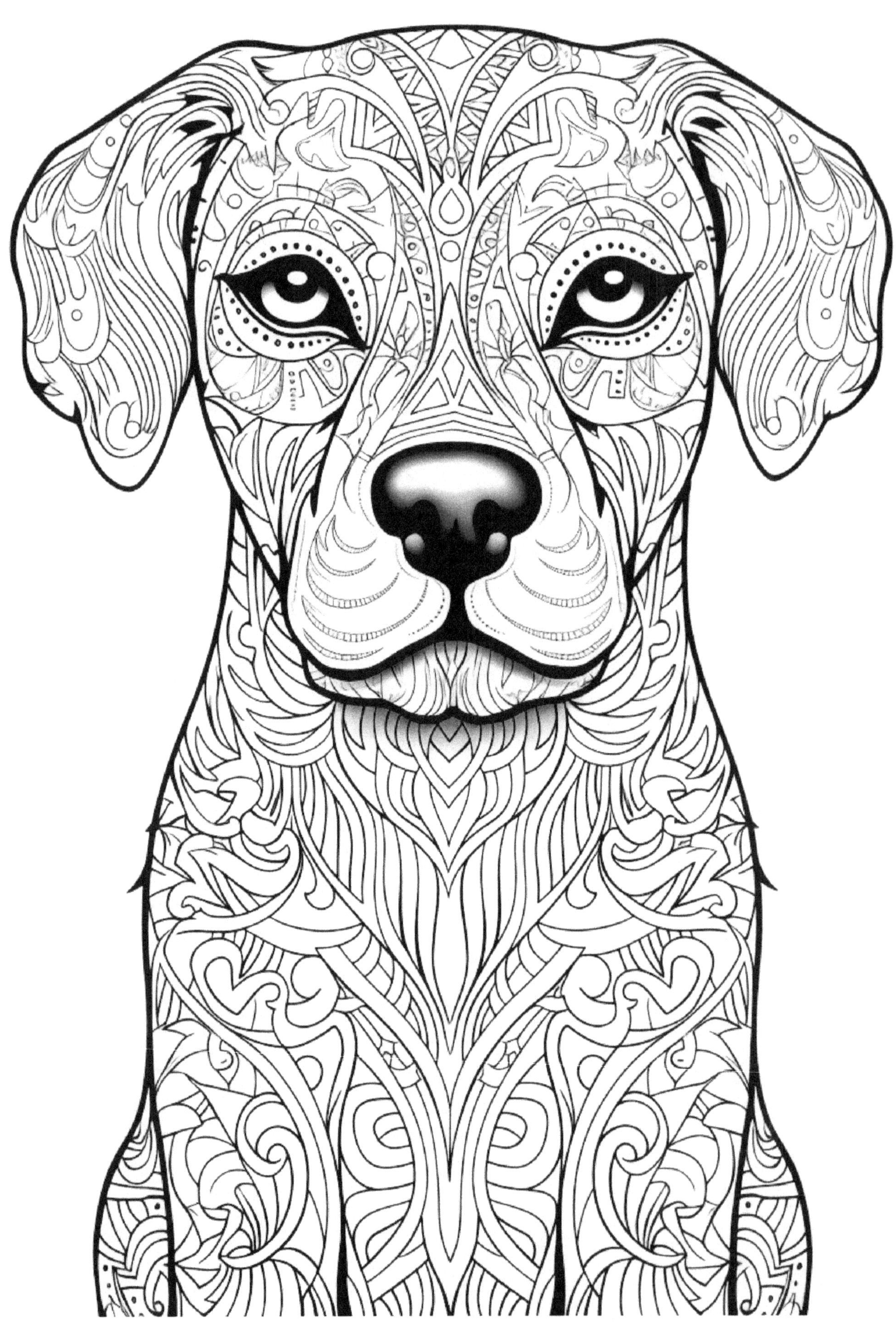

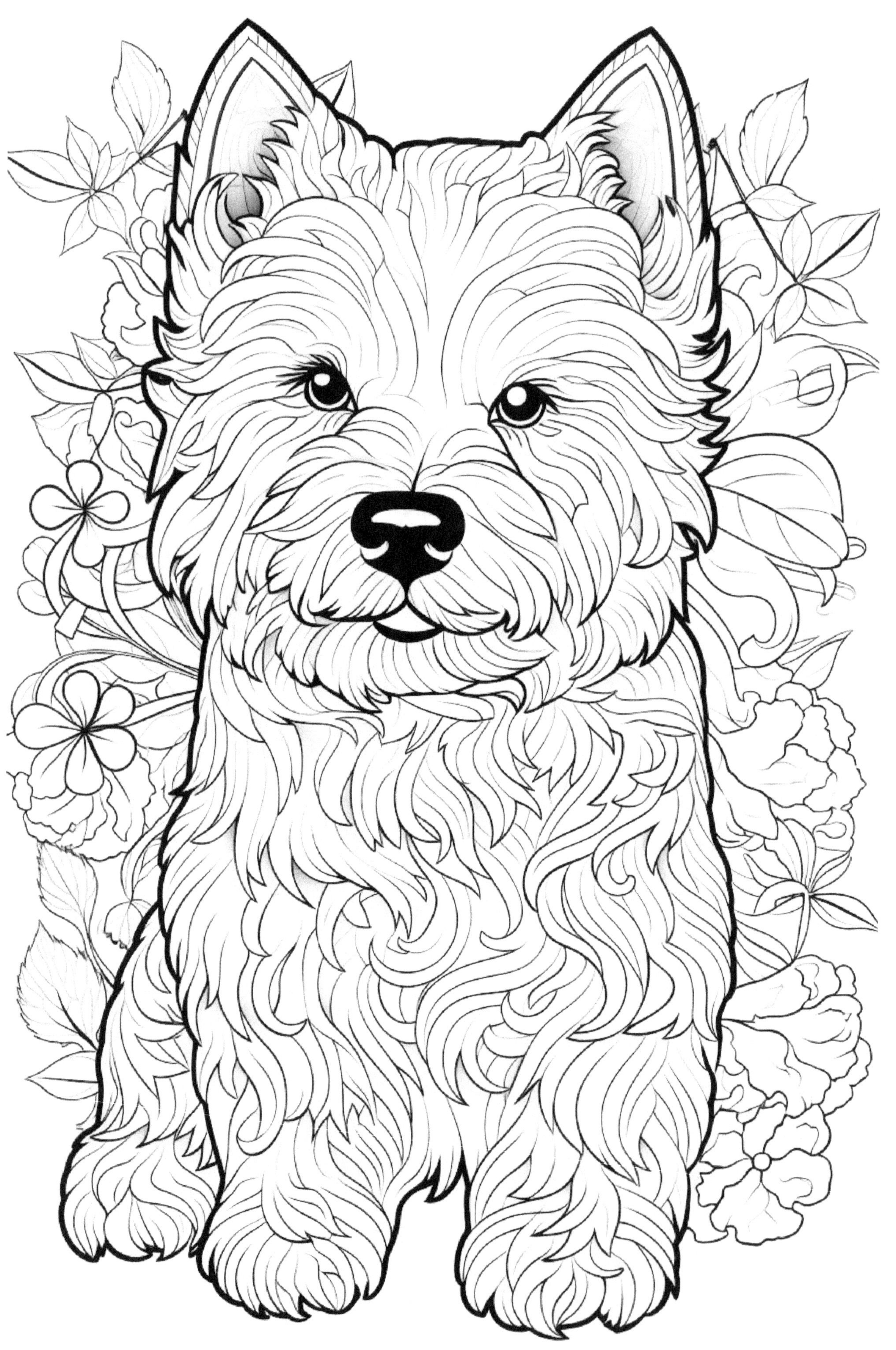

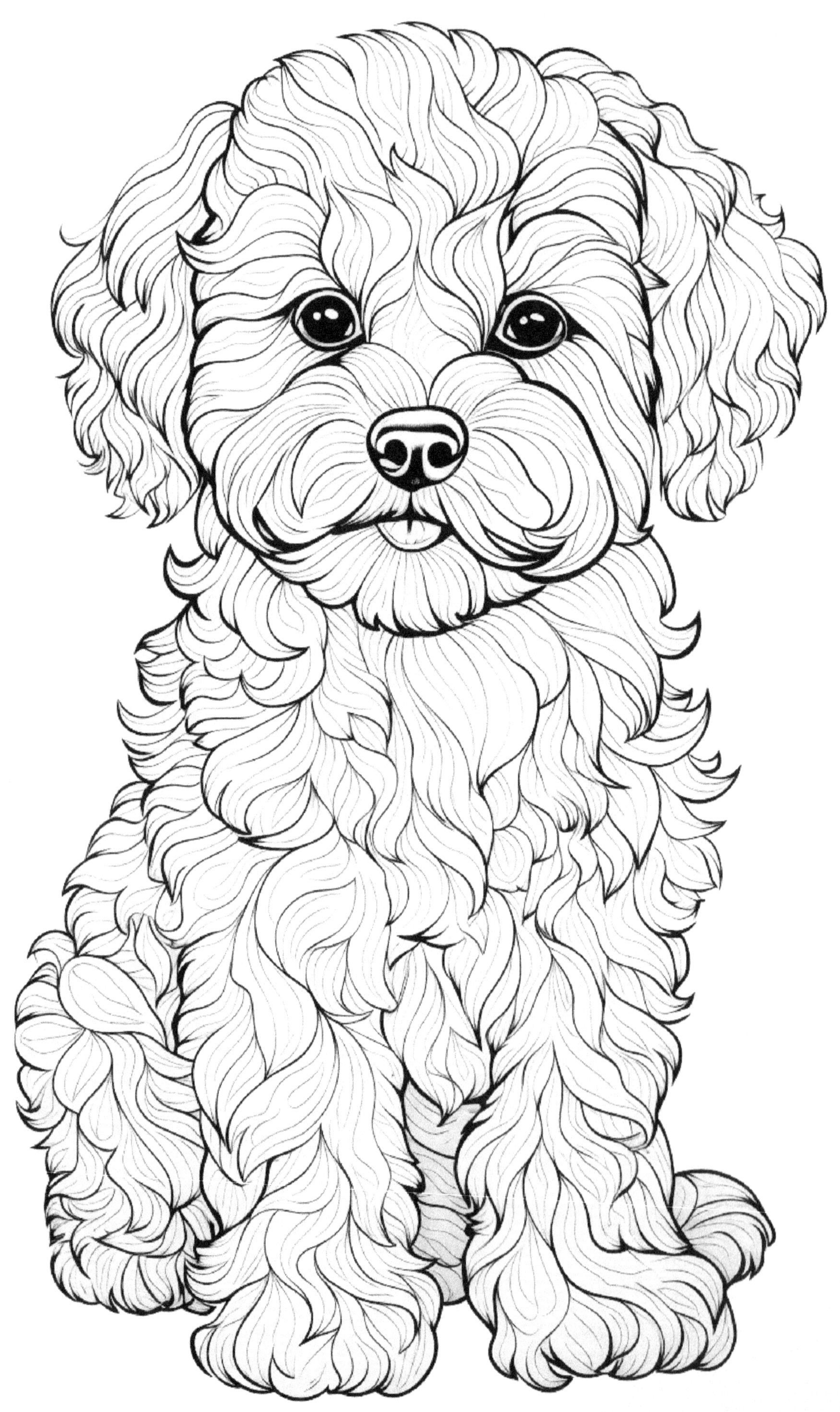

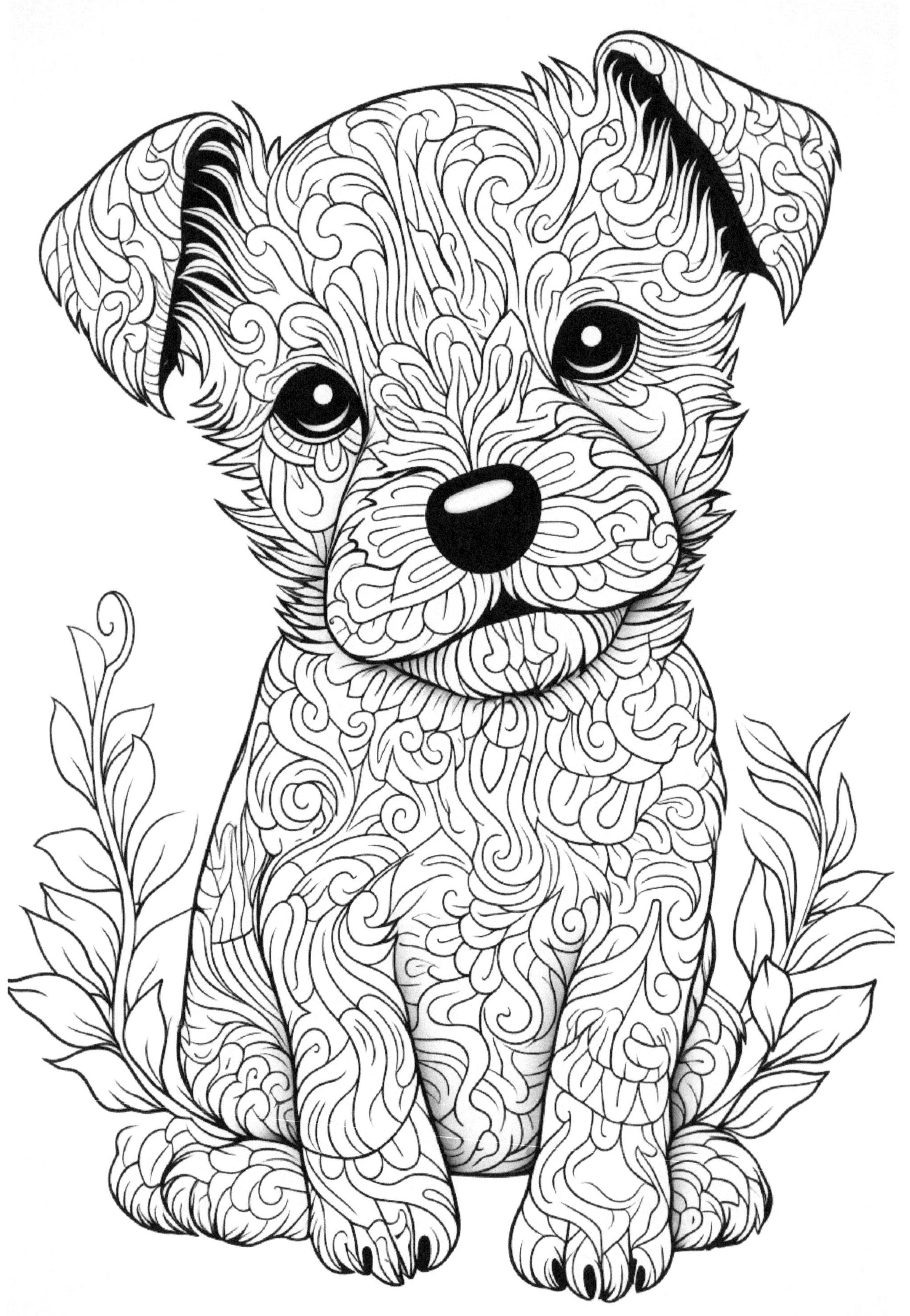

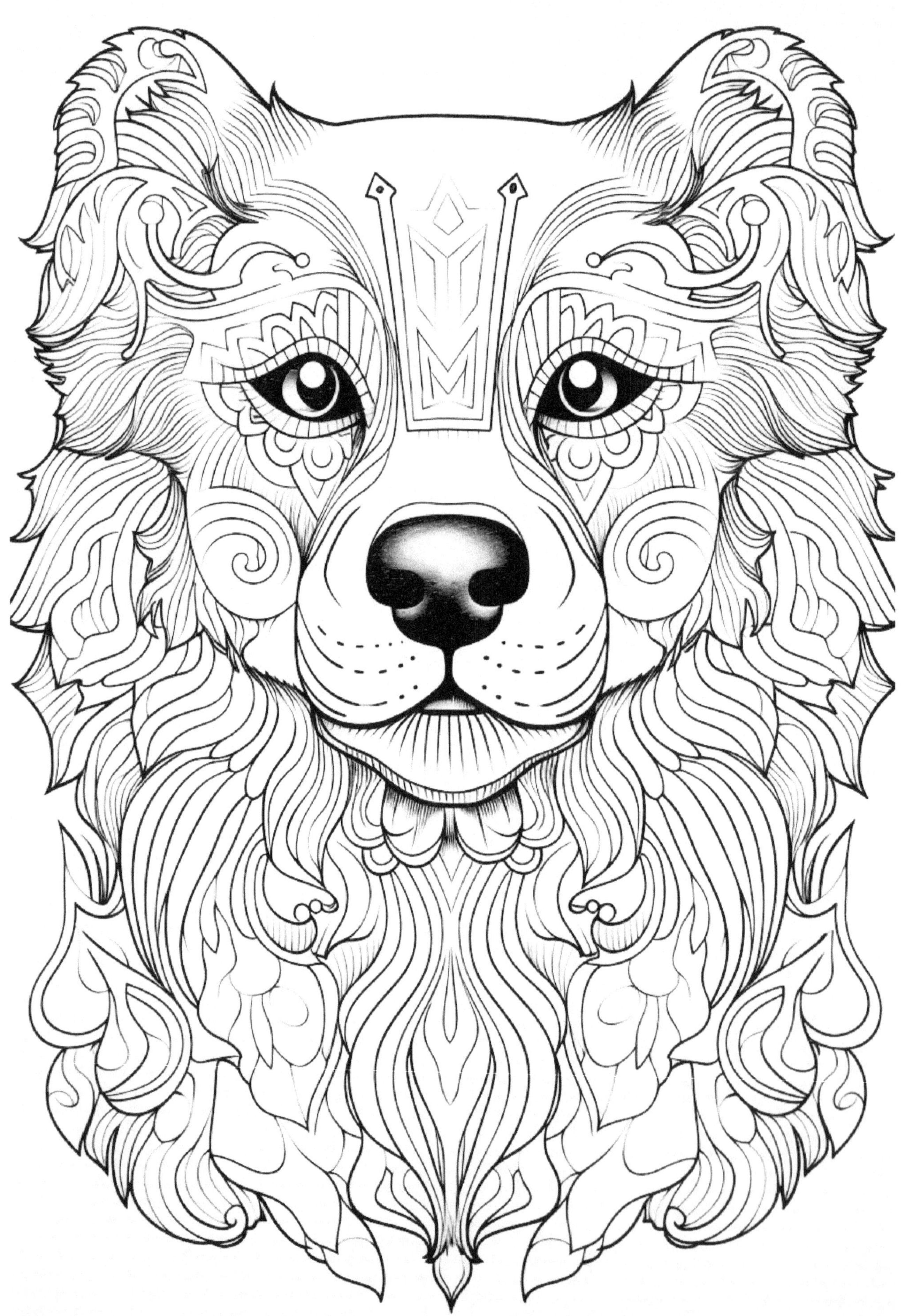

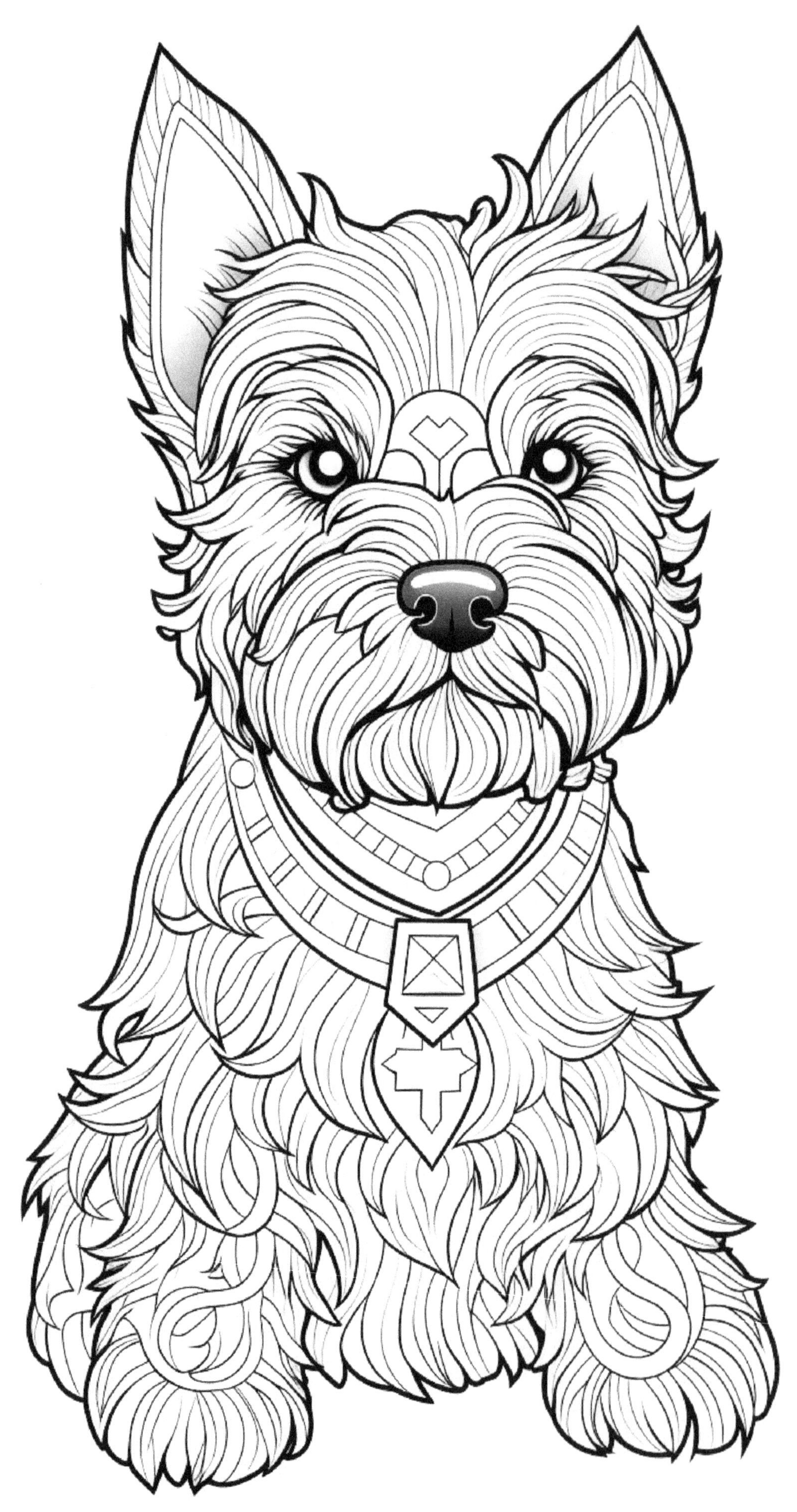

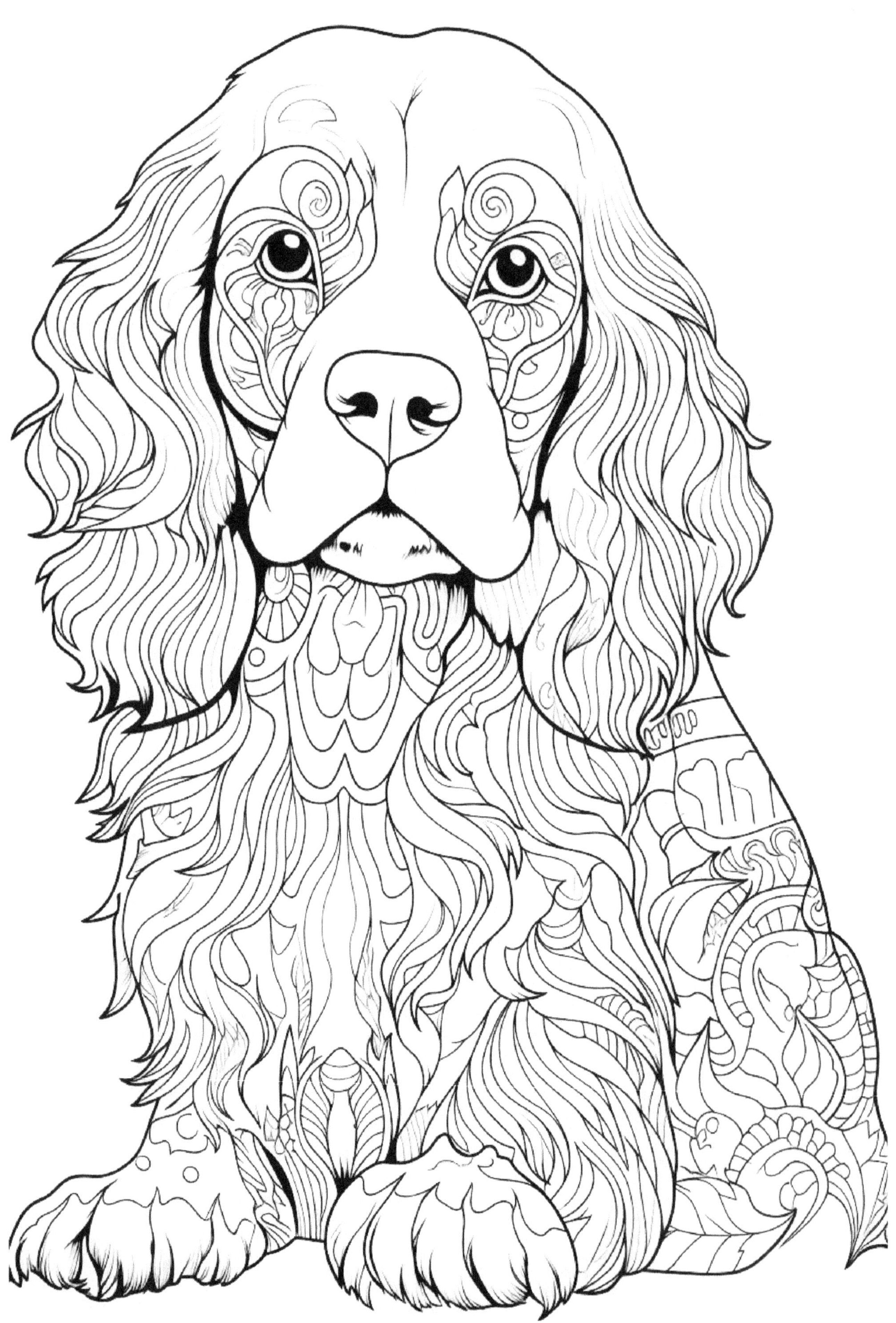

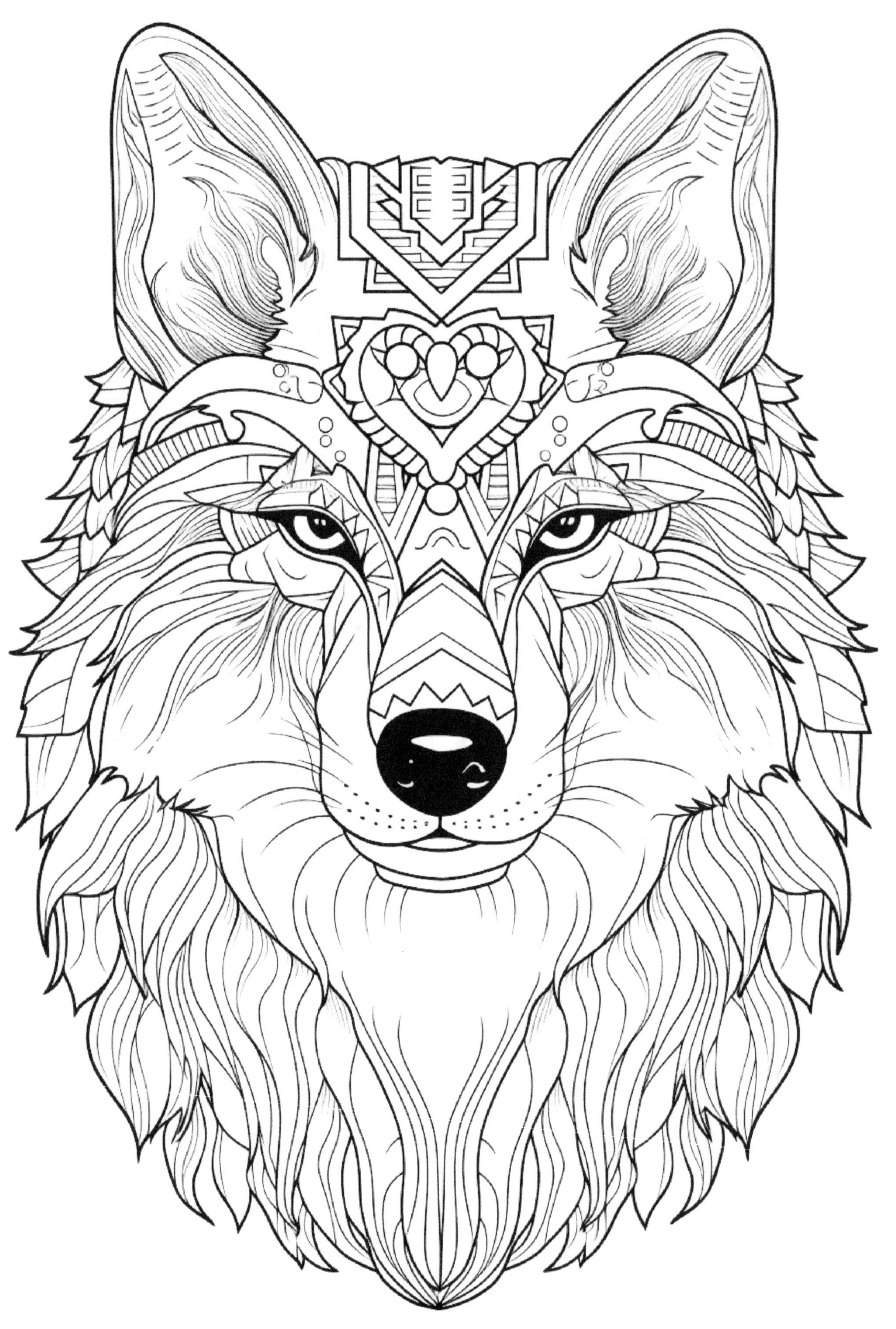

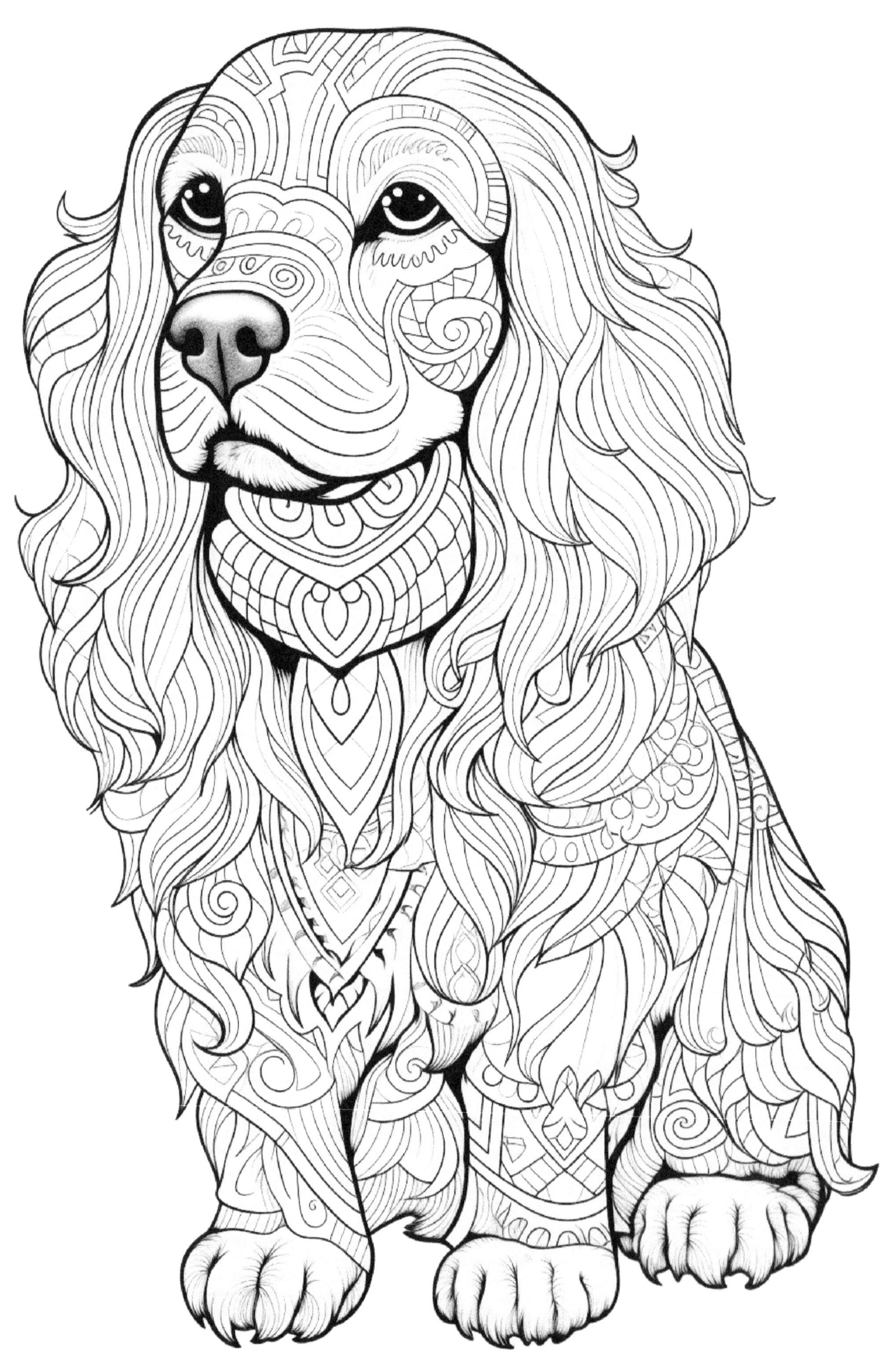

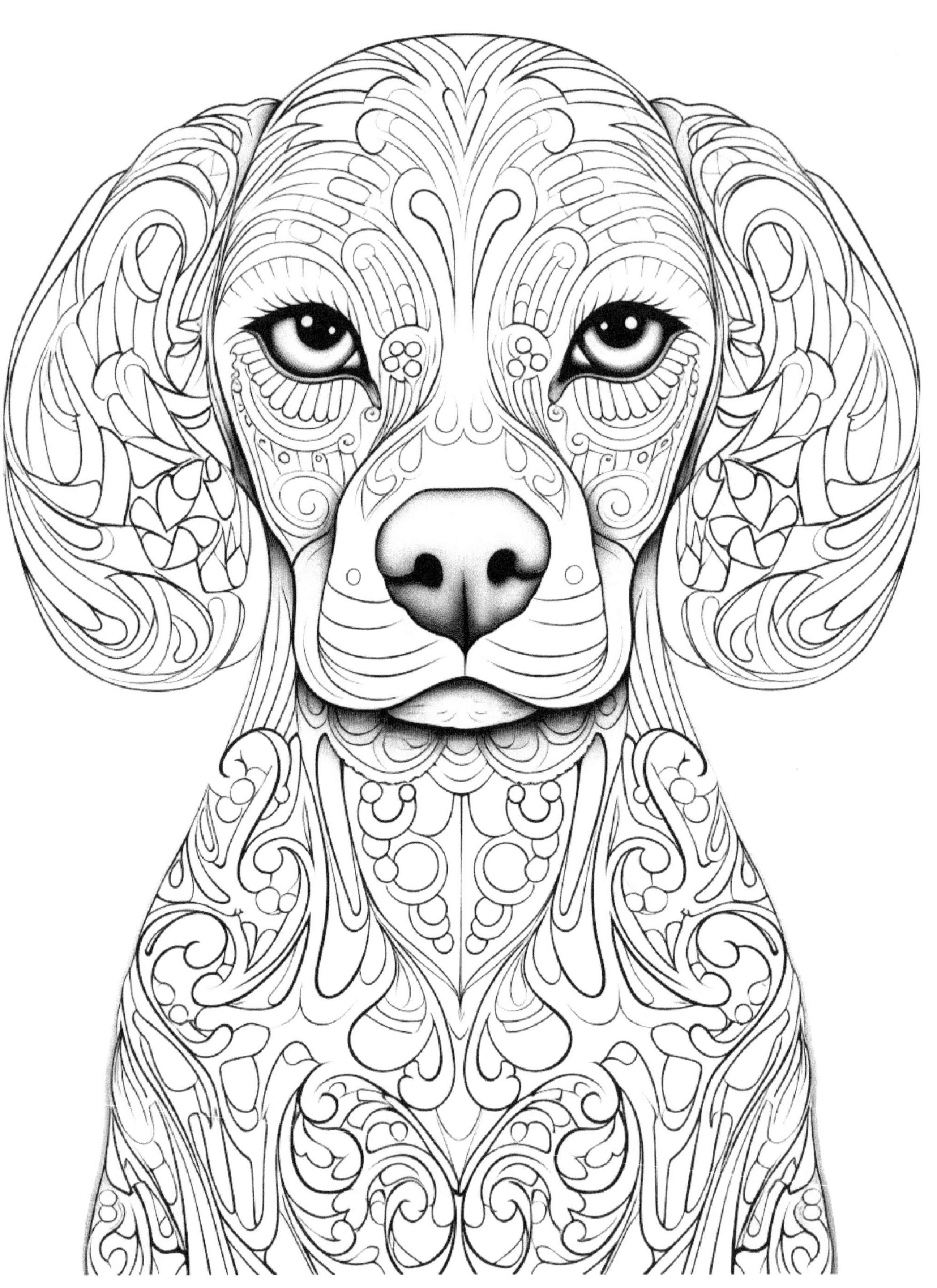

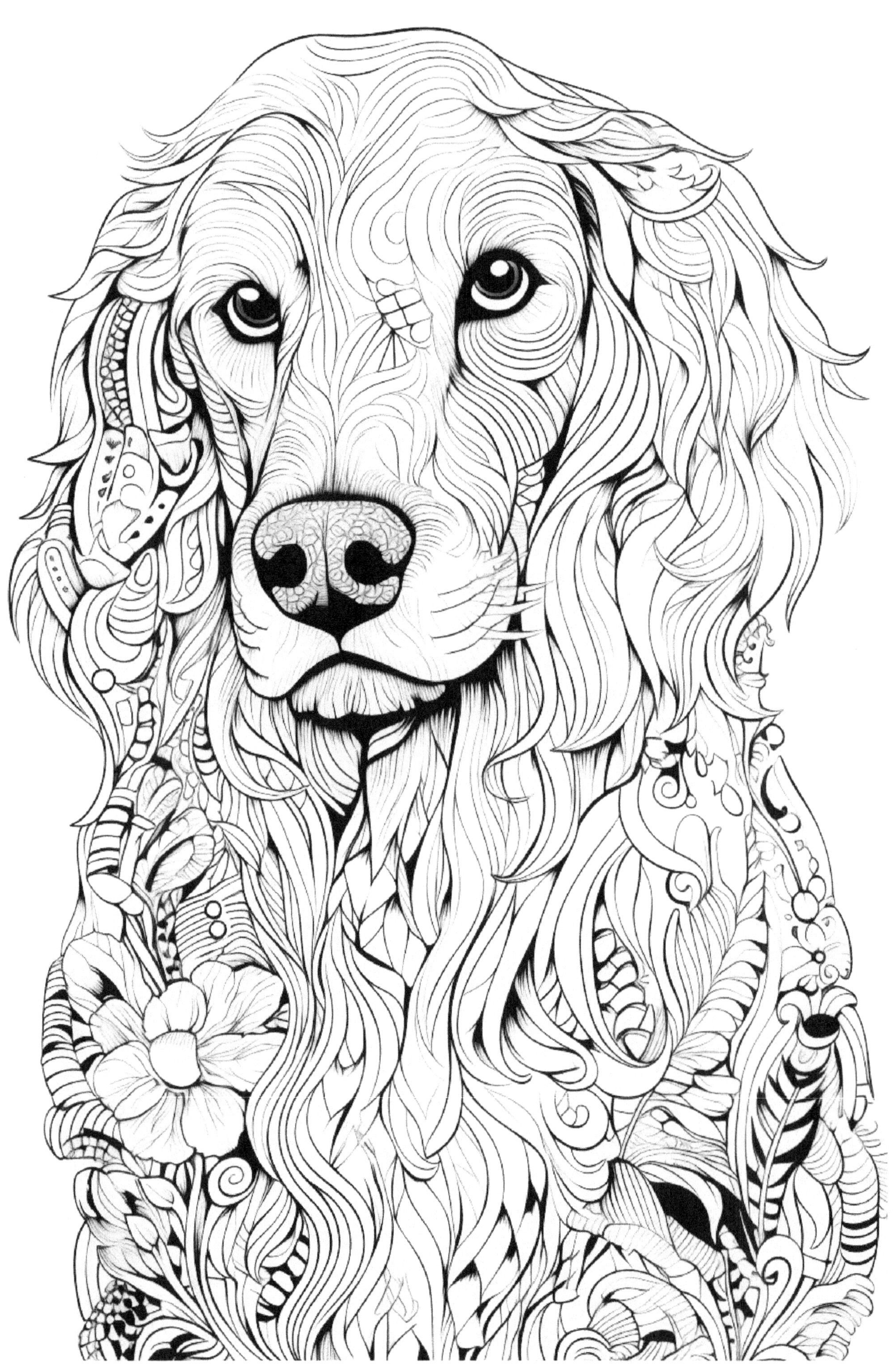

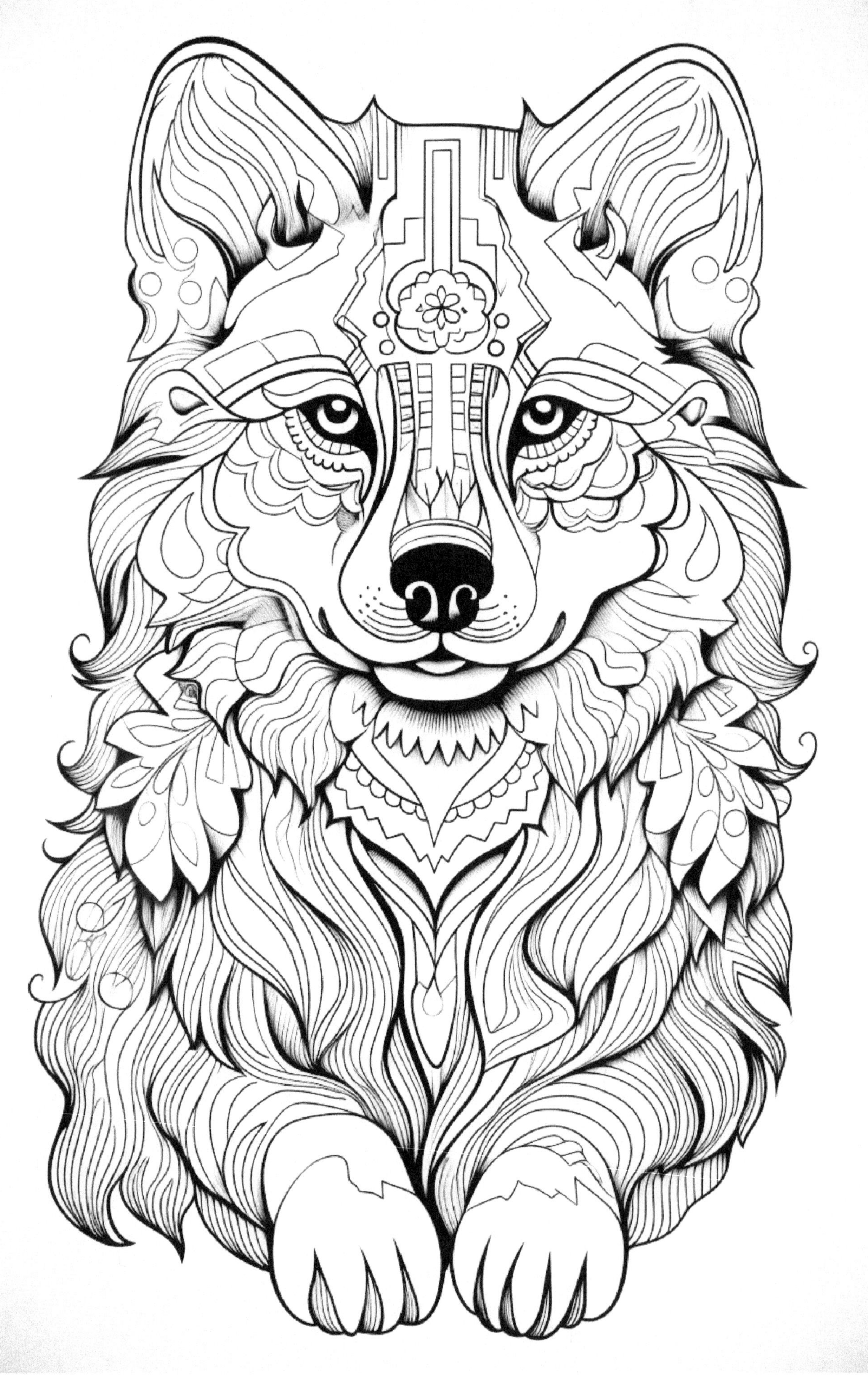

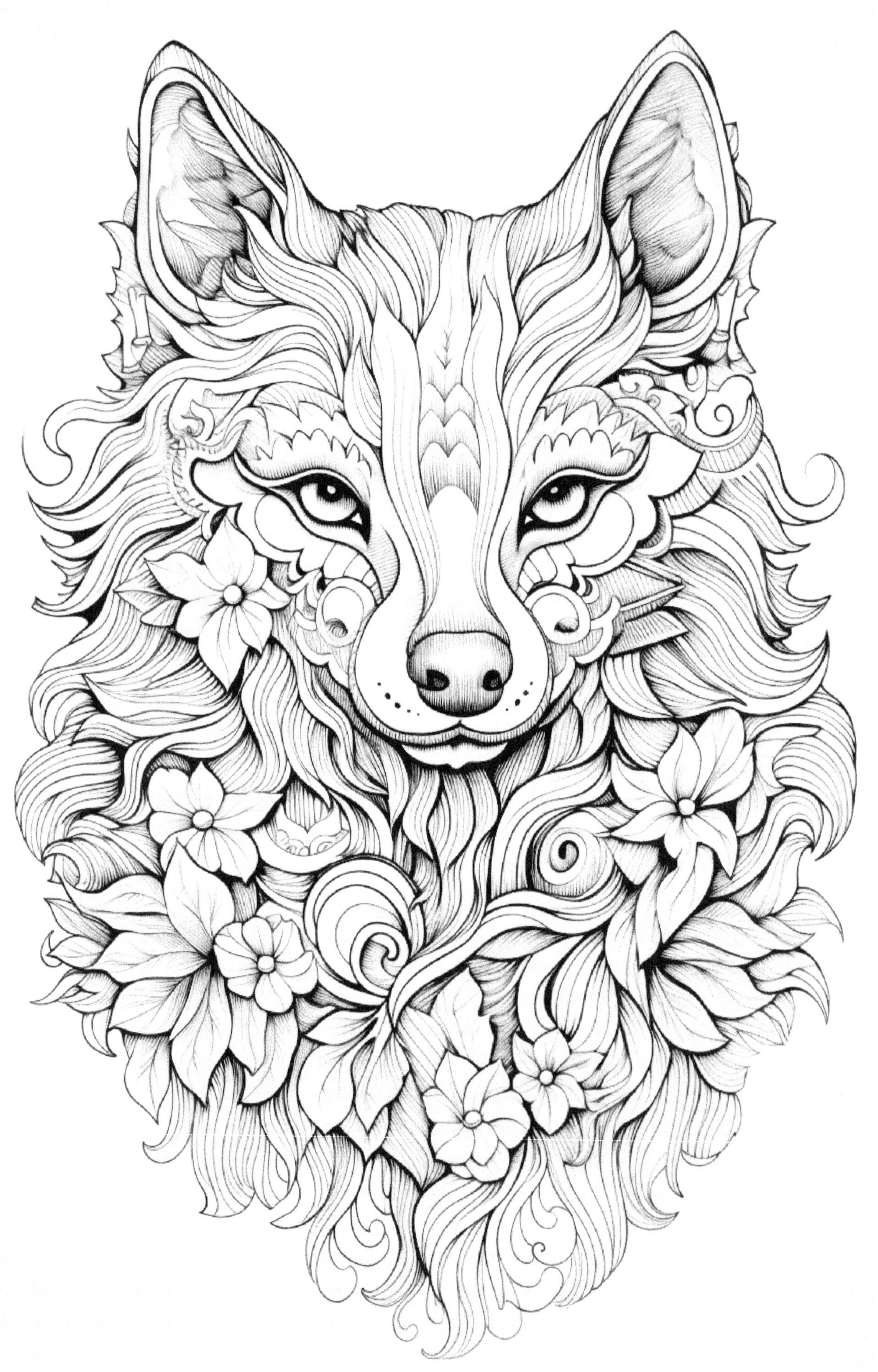

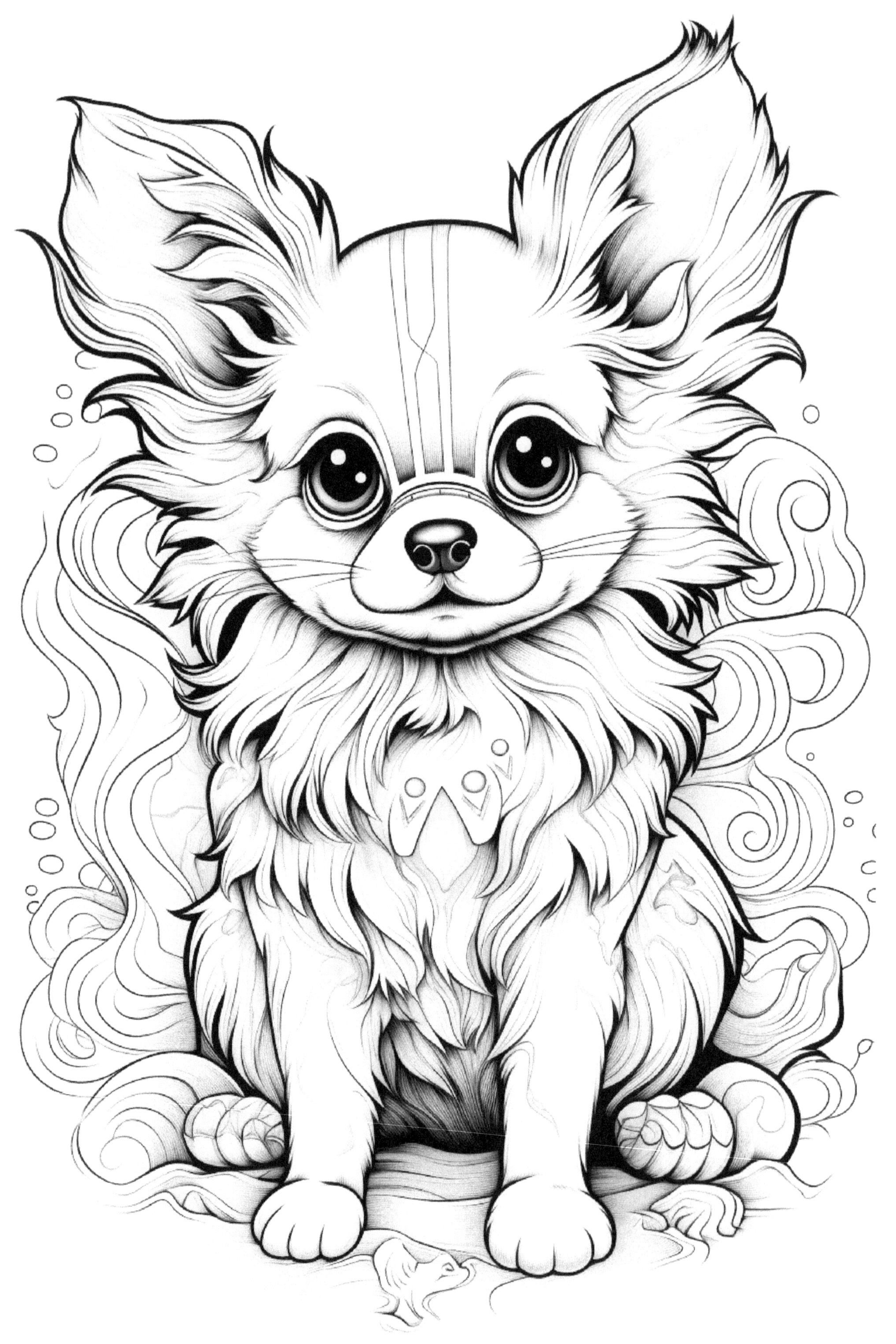